My Beautiful Life

Manifesting All of God's Blessings In Your Life

Dr. Chibundo Marchie

My Beautiful Life

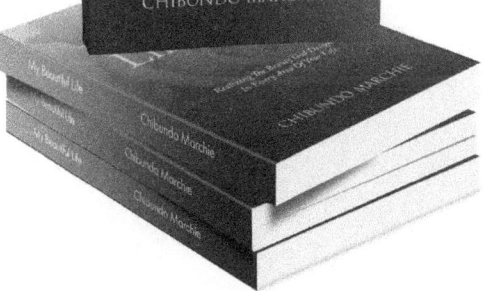

My Beautiful Life

REHOBOTH HOUSETM

Copyright © 2020 by Dr. Chibundo Marchie

My Beautiful Life

ISBN: 978-1-64301-019-9

Unless otherwise indicated, all scripture quotations are taken from the Authorized King James Version of the Holy Bible (KJV).

The opinions expressed by the author in this book are exclusively hers and not of Rehoboth House. *Contact Dr. Chibundo for counseling, teachings, seminars, and workshops.*

Book Available Online
www.amazon.com
www.barnesandnoble.com
www.gimfglobal.org
Other Major Online Bookstores

Contact For Enquiries
Call: 804-502-1926
Email:chibundoanene@yahoo.com

Author's Contact
Email: chibundoanene@yahoo.com

Published By Rehoboth House, Chicago
Email: info@rehobothhouseonline.com
www. rehobothhouseonline.com

Cover And Interior Design
Rehoboth House, Chicago

Printed in the United States of America, April 2020

REHOBOTH HOUSE

My Beautiful Life

Contents

Introduction..ix

Chapter 1

FELLOWSHIP FOR BEAUTY..1

Chapter 2

RADIATING HIS BEAUTY...13

Chapter 3

TRANSFERRING OF BEAUTY......................................21

Chapter 4

VISION FOR BEAUTY..31

Chapter 5

MARITAL BEAUTY..49

Chapter 6

CREATING YOUR BEAUTY: POWER OF SPOKEN WORD.........57

Chapter 7

ENFORCING YOUR BEAUTY: OBEDIENCE..............75

Chapter 8

FAITH IS ALL IT TAKES..87

Chapter 9

FAITH ANTAGONIST I: HINDRANCES TO BEAUTY............95

Chapter 10

FAITH ANTAGONISTS II...105

My Beautiful Life

Introduction

What Do I Mean By Beautiful Life?

The blessing of God beautifies a man; so, by a beautiful life, I mean a life that is blessed and manifesting God's promises and glory. Therefore, get set to be decorated with your desires for your beauty for the glory of God. Beauty is God's plan for you because you are His child.

> *"No good thing will God hold from them that walk uprightly"* **(Psalm 87:1).**

God delights in beautifying His children as a father delights in beautifying his children. Let it never come to your mind that God is withholding a blessing from you, no, it is His will to grant your desires.

> *"Little Children, it is your Father's pleasure to give you the kingdom"* **(Luke 12:32).**

This is to assure you that your desire is obtainable. Be confident that God is willing to give you your desire, is the first step towards receiving from God; this is faith.

Faith Is The Foundation Of A Beautiful Life

> *"Now faith is the substance of things hoped for, the evidence of things not seen"* (Heb.11:2).

Without faith, you cannot receive from God. Do you need healing? Be confident that God is willing and able to do it. Do you need a Wife or Husband? Believe God is willing and able. This applies to any and every blessing you desire, such as academic excellence, marital breakthrough, finance, ministry, etc. With God all your desires are possible. Being in the kingdom of God is likened to a tree planted by rivers of water. In this kingdom, everything you need for a glorious life is available and obtainable.

CHAPTER 1

Fellowship For Beauty

Like I said in the introduction, the first step to a beautiful life is faith, the confident assurance that God is willing and able to grant your desires.

The next step is asking, and this brings us to this Chapter; fellowship for Beauty. Fellowship simply means relationship. If you need something from God or anyone, relationship (fellowship) is important. Someone might have what you need, but you would not know until you relate to him. Until there is a relationship, you will not receive.

Relationship Is Necessary For Receiving From God

Next question is how do I fellowship or relate to God? You relate to God through communication. Every relationship is based on communication. Have you noticed that when communication goes bad, relationships go sour? And this is why bad communicators are rarely good friends.

> *"They look unto him; they were enlightened and not ashamed"* (Psalms 34:5).

Looking into Him' connotes a relationship. When you are in a relationship with God through Christ, trusting, relying, and depending on Him, you will not be ashamed. Your face will be lightened up; beautified. If you desire a beautiful life that manifests the fullness of God's blessing, let your relationship with him be strong. Never allow anything to hinder your relationship and communication with Him.

I tell you unless you allow it, nothing is strong enough to separate you from God or break your communication with Him. The disciples said to Jesus in John 6:68, "Where do we go from you; you have the word of life." No matter the challenges you are facing never consider quitting.

> *Job says even if he slays me, I shall trust Him. David said, "Who do I have in heaven, but you or who do I desire on earth, but you."When challenges come, cling to Him.*

Anything that cuts your fellowship with God is setting you up for shame and disgrace. As long as your eyes are on Him, you will never be ashamed.

As long as the disciples were with Jesus, fellowshipping with Him, they lacked nothing and were not sick. The Israelites lacked nothing in the wilderness because of the presence of God. Until you break fellowship with him, you may not appreciate the benefits of his presence.

God is not your problem or foe; He is never against you or trying to catch you. The devil is your problem and your accuser. When you seek the Lord, you obtain His power and glory for a beautiful life. If you keep friendship with God, His power will work for your beauty.

Relating To God Has Two Dimensions:

- Corporate Fellowship

- Personal fellowship

Corporate Fellowship

Corporate fellowship simply means fellowshipping with other believers as you see in Church worship.

> *"Where two or three are gathered in my name I am the midst of them"* (Matthew 18:20).

There are blessings reserved for corporate fellowship.

> *"Not forsaking the assembling of ourselves together, as the manner of some is; but exhorting one another: and so much the more, as ye see the day approaching"* (Hebrew 10:25).

Personal Fellowship

Personal fellowship in this context is referring to your fellowship alone with God. The basis of this type of fellowship with God is communication. Whichever type of communication, it is two ways; from you to God and from God to you.

Major Ways You Can Communicate With God

- Praying the Word

- Praise and Worship

Major Ways God Uses In Communicating With You

- Through His Word

- The leading of the Holy Spirit

Prayer

Praying is communicating with God through prayer

> *"If ye abide in me, and my words abide in you, ye shall ask what ye will, and it shall be done unto you"* **(John 15: 7).**

It does not matter the kind of relationship you have with people that have what you need if you do not ask, you will not receive. God is rich in all things, but you have to ask to receive.

Luke 15:28-31 has a lesson for everyone. The brother of the prodigal son had a wealthy father as well but lived in denial because he did not ask. When a need arises in your life; open your mouth and ask God. When challenges come to mar your beauty, do not keep quiet and watch. Arise and cry out. Cry out for God's intervention like the blind Bartimaeus. Whether small or big, if it needs God, ask. Let nothing break your prayer. Let nothing be too big or too small to ask. Without asking Him, you can receive nothing.

No one receives anything; except that which is given Him from Heaven. When devil breaks your prayer life, he mars your beauty. Prayer is drawing down God's hands and powers from heaven to intervene on earth.

> *"That poor man cried, and God answered, and saved him out of all his troubles"* **(Psalm 34:6)**.

If a poor man prayed, everyone could pray. Prayer is not expensive and is free. We all have free access to God, by the blood of Jesus. Anyone can pray, and God will hear.

When you pray, God responds. God does not store prayer; He answers prayers. Jesus while on earth demonstrated God's willingness to answer prayer. He never turned down a request. If you care to pray, God will answer. This is the confidence you should have in your prayer. That when you pray, God answers.

> *"And this is the confidence that we have in him, that, if we ask anything according to his will, he heareth us"* **(1 John 5:14).**

God says as you have spoken in His ears, so shall He do.

> *"And it shall come to pass, that before they call, I will answer; and while they are still speaking, I will answer" "Prayer is as simple as that; talking to God, God hearing and performing"* **(Isaiah 65:14).**

Today, many for one reason or the other have lost confidence in prayer and resorted to complaining and begging. I rather beg God than men.

> *"I will lift up mine eyes unto the hills, from whence cometh my help. My help cometh from the LORD, which made heaven and earth"* **(Psalm 121:1-2).**

When you pray, God uses any means to answer your prayer. He is the source and can use any means He chooses. God does not grudge He does exceedingly above what you ask. When you ask men, you limit yourself. Your help comes from God the maker and owner of heaven and earth and everyone in it. Whatever need you have, be it emotional, psychological, material, etc., Ask God and look up to Him as your only source.

Refuse anything that will make you look at man for help. If God does not do it, you do not need it yet, its time has not come. Refuse to cut corners.

> *"Every good gift and every perfect gift is from above, and cometh down from the Father of lights, with whom is no variableness, neither shadow of turning"* **(James 1:17).**

Rebuild your prayer life. Ask even for the least. Enough of shame and begging. Just like one eye cannot look up and the other look down, you cannot look up to God and man at the same time, choose one.

Praise And Worship

After praying, believe you receive and give Him thanks. You believe after praying, and then you receive. Believing, proceeds receiving. This is why thanksgiving should follow every objective prayer. Do not wait to receive, before thanking. If you believe, you receive, you should then give thanks, before the desire manifests. What do you do in between believing and receiving, you give thanks, praise, and worship.

When you prayed, and the burden is lifted, you have prayed through; the next step is to praise and worship.

> *"Be careful for nothing; but in everything by prayer and supplication with thanksgiving let your requests be made known unto God"* **(Philippians 4:6).**

Praise and worship is the quickest way to get divine intervention. Praise and worship bring the manifestation of your desires. If you live a life of praise and worship, God will decorate you with His beauty and glory.

When you worship Him, His glory and power rub on you for beauty. Wake up every day with praise and worship, and you will experience a dramatic turnaround for your beauty. His beauty replaces every ugliness. God inhabits the praises of his people. When you praise and worship God, you become His abode, and everything in your life is transformed. Also, lack is terminated.

> *"Ye shall have a song, as in the night when a holy solemnity is kept; and gladness of heart, as when one goeth with a pipe to come into the mountain of the LORD, to the mighty One of Israel"* (Isaiah 30:29).

Fellowshipping with God is two ways, you talking to God and God talking back to you. God talks to you through His word and the leading of the Holy Spirit, and you talk to Him through praise and worship.

We shall be discussing God communicating with us through His word in the next chapter.

Leading Of The Holy Spirit

> *"But God hath revealed them unto us by his Spirit: for the Spirit searcheth all things, yea, the deep things of God. For what man knoweth the things of a man, save the spirit of man which is in him? Even so, the things of God knoweth no man, but the Spirit of God. Now we have received, not the spirit of the world, but the spirit which is of God; that we might know the things that are freely given to us of God"* (1 Corinthians 2:10-12).

The Spirit of God knows the mind of God and communicates it to you. This is the leading of the Holy Spirit. The Spirit of God reveals the mind of the father, so you can please Him and maintain a good fellowship. Nothing ruins fellowships than offenses. The leading of the Holy Spirit helps you not to offend God and grow in fellowship with Him.

> *"He restoreth my soul: he leadeth me in the paths of righteousness for his name's sake"* **(Psalm 23:3).**

When your fellowship with God is unhindered, blessings flow to you continually for your beauty. If you must maximize beauty, then surrender completely to the leading of the Holy Spirit.

It should be God's will and not your will. In denying self and following Him, not only does the Holy Spirit help you to please God, but He also guides you to where your blessings are. When you pray, praise and worship, God releases your blessing and expects you to gather them through the leading of His Spirit. The Holy Spirit guides you to where your blessings are to gather them.

> *"That **thou givest them they gather: thou openest thine hand, they are filled with good"*** **(Psalm 104:28).**

The Holy Spirit Guides You To Your Blessings

If Simeon in Luke 2:25-32 was not guided by the Holy Spirit, he would have missed his blessing of seeing the Messiah. If you allow the Holy Spirit lead you, He will guide you to hidden treasures for your life to be beautiful. Allow God to lead you by His spirit for your good. You may not understand His leading, just obey. When the Israelites cried; God released Manna and instructed them where to find them. They could have missed it if they did not obey.

Today many are crying for the blessing that has already been released. Their problem is either ignorance or disobedience to the leading of the Holy Spirit, refusing to obey that thought, desire or plan God put in their hearts. As you pray, watch. Watch (be sensitive) to the leading of the Holy Spirit. You have to be sensitive as you pray, because the leading of the Holy Spirit may come as a flash, a thought, an idea or an impression. You have to be sensitive to grasp it, whichever way it comes.

Prayer focus should be more on understanding the leading of the Holy Spirit. Prayers like "What do I do Lord for my blessing" "Where do I go and which way." God leads you to every blessing. The Holy Spirit positions and prepares you for your blessing.

> *"He maketh me to lie down in green pastures: he leadeth me beside the still waters. He restoreth my soul: he leadeth me in the paths of righteousness for his name's sake" (Ps. 23: 2-3).*

> *"For as many as are led by the Spirit of God, they are the sons of God" (Romans 8:14).*

Until the Holy Spirit leads you, you are not a bonafide Son of God. Only Sons are heirs of their Father. When as a son of God you are led by the Holy Spirit you reap blessing and beauty. May God grant you insight to your blessing; what to do and where to go for it. All you need for your beautiful life is already released only be led to it by the Holy Spirit.

> *"Blessed be the God and Father of our Lord Jesus Christ, which according to his abundant mercy hath begotten us again unto a lively hope by the resurrection of Jesus Christ from the dead" (1 Peter 1:3).*

God is not stringy or hoarding money, breakthroughs, cars, houses, wife, husband, marital blessing, etc. He does not need anything you may desire in heaven; they are all here for you.

I command your eyes to be open to see his leading in Jesus Mighty Name. Amen!!

> *"And thine ears shall hear a word behind thee, saying, This is the way, walk ye in it when ye turn to the right hand, and when ye turn to the left" (Isaiah 30:21).*

Treasures are hidden in secret places, but He reveals them and gives them to us by His leading. Jesus by the leading of the Holy Spirit was never stranded. The Bible records that Jesus Himself knew what to do in every situation. He was never stranded. When they needed money to pay tax, He knew the exact place to go. He knew the exact accommodation for the Passover feasts.

Check His earthly ministry; He had a solution to every problem, need or want. When you cultivate the leading of the

Holy Spirit, you will save yourself, needless hours of prayer (Vain repetitions).

Man's resistance to change is his greatest enemy to the leading of the Spirit, and this hinders his blessing. Most times the Holy Spirit will lead you to something new. Love and embrace change for your blessing and beauty. Whatever God puts in your heart to do, be excited to do it, even if it is something new.

> *"And whatsoever ye do, do it heartily, as to the Lord, and not unto men" (Colossians 3:23).*

When you keep doing the same thing in the same way; you have the same result. If you do not like what you have and how your life is, allow the Holy Spirit to lead you to something different and be willing to do it for your good. Your husband or wife to be might be sitting on the other side of the church, just obey that prompting to change your seat. You must not take the same route to work every day or shop in the same mall always. Allow the Holy Spirit lead you to something new and different.

> *"For I know the thoughts that I think toward you, saith the LORD, thoughts of peace, and not of evil, to give you an expected end"* (Jeremiah 29:11).

Allow Him to lead you to that good thought and plan He has for your life.

CHAPTER 2

Radiating His Beauty

The word of God is an integral part of our fellowship with Him. It is the means God uses to communicate with us. The place and role of God's word in beauty cannot be overemphasised:

The word enables you to discover and acquire. You discover what is yours in the word and acquire them by the same word. The word is the path to your blessing. **(See Josh 1: 8, 2 Peter 1: 3, Proverb 24: 13-14).** You will not know that healing is yours until you discover that from the word. And that same word tells you how to obtain that healing.

The word builds your faith to obtain your blessing. **(See Romans10:17, Hebrew11:2, Acts 20: 32).** When you hear and study God's word concerning a specific blessing, faith is developed for you to obtain it.

God's word makes you radiate His beauty. The essence of the relationship is not only to receive but to manifest and represent the other person. God's word makes you more like Him. In a close and intimate relationship, life is transferred, shared and manifested. You are impacted by a relationship to reveal the other. This is why it is so important to choose your relationship wisely. You are who you hang out with.

> *"Be not deceived: evil communications corrupt good manners"* **(1 Corinthians 15: 33).**

More than just the blessing, God wants you to reveal Him to the world, so that the world may know Him. In fact, this is the major reason he brought you into fellowship with Himself. We are the only one God has chosen to manifest Himself through. The reason God is blessing you is to reveal Himself. **(1 Peter 2: 9).** You are of no value to the kingdom if you have all the big houses and cars and not in any way reveal God to others. God is not pleased if you do not manifest His nature, power, and authority. You are merely an addition to the "Rich" people in the world if you do not manifest God.

What should differentiate you from the other rich person who does not have Christ is not the car you drive, the house you live in, your grades in school, the dresses you wear or your shoes, but the presence and nature of God that you manifest (let out or project). People in the world do not know who God is, and God has brought you into a relationship to reveal Himself; His beauty to the world. There is no ugliness in God, so manifesting Him, means manifesting beauty.

Jesus, God's begotten son, had a relationship with God before He came to earth. And when He came, He revealed the Father to the world.

> *"Believest thou not that I am in the Father, and the Father in me? The words that I speak unto you I speak not of myself: but the Father that dwelleth in me, he doeth the works. Believe me that I* **am** *in the Father, and the Father in me: or else believe me for the very works' sake"* (**John 14: 10-11**).

Jesus manifested the fullness of God; His full beauty. Jesus is the express image of God. He manifested all that God is. And the same way God intends that when people see you, their search for Him would be met. This means that you give them the love and help of God.

Jesus is Emmanuel, God with us; meeting our search for God. To what extent do you meet people's search for God? Do you meet their problems and answer their questions, or do you compound their issues? Do you through God's love make life easier for them? You may not do for them the so much as God would, but you can do the least that you have received grace for. After Jesus left, the disciples were recognized to have been with Him, adding value to lives.

> *"Now when they saw the boldness of Peter and John and perceived that they were unlearned and ignorant men, they marvelled; and they took knowledge of them, that they had been with Jesus"* (**Acts 4:13**).

The disciples had fellowship with Jesus for three years, got impacted and manifested it when He left. If you have a genuine relationship with Jesus, you are expected to manifest Him and do the works He did, even greater. **(John 14:12)** Jesus died young, so you can live all your long days manifesting Him for greater works. You are not living for yourself.

"Whether we live or die it is for Christ" **(Romans 14:8).**

How much time do you need for people to recognize you have been with Jesus; that you are in a relationship with Him? When will you start doing His works; talking His word, going His places, etc. As the father has sent Jesus, so He has sent you. God does not expect less work from you than Jesus did.

Moses of the old covenant encountered God only for forty days and radiated His glory, in so much that people could not come near him. Could it be the reason people are always on your case; troubling you is that you are not radiating His glory yet?

"When a man's way pleases the Lord, He makes His enemies at peace with Him" **(Proverbs 16:7).**

Paul says trouble me not for I bear on my body the mark of Christ. Radiating God's beauty is a shield from trouble. Most trouble that people have is what they caused for themselves by their lawlessness. He that walks in the light has no occasion to stumble. Your fellowship with the father is questionable if you do not radiate Him in your talk, works, at school, mall, walk, in dressing, and everywhere you go.

God's word enables you to radiate Him. The word of God is God Himself; God's will and nature. As you read and study the word, you are relating to God, and His nature rubs off on you. You do not struggle to radiate Him, only fix your eyes on the word and you will see your life transformed before your eyes.

> *"But we all, with open face beholding as in a glass the glory of the Lord, are changed into the same image from glory to glory, even as by the Spirit of the Lord."* **(2 Cor. 3:18)**

The Word is like a Mirror. Just as the physical mirror perfects your physical beauty, the word of God touches your inner beauty, which radiates out. The word adds colours of virtue to you. If you look continuously to this mirror, you are charged from glory to glory by the Spirit.

Today you may seem far from manifesting Him, do not be discouraged and give up. Keep in the mirror of the word; very soon you will be manifesting Him. And people will hardly recognize you, because of His power and glory in your life.

Enhance your beauty, by the mirror of God's word. Anything ungodly in your life is liable to change by the transforming power of the word. Mend any ugliness in your life by doing issue-oriented study. Fear is ugly; replace it as you study on faith. Hate is ugly and should be replaced by studying love.

> *"And be not conformed to this world: but be ye transformed by the renewing of your mind, that ye may prove what is that good, and acceptable, and perfect, will of God"* **(Rom. 12:2).**

The word is both the makeup and cosmetologist. All the beauty (nature) of God is in the word, and the Holy Spirit puts them on you, as you study the word. Whenever you look at the physical mirror, ask yourself; have you looked at the mirror of the word? What happens to your natural beauty if you do not look at the physical mirror also happens to the glory of God's you radiate if you do not read the Bible. As natural beauty is observed and maintained by a physical mirror, likewise, God's beauty you radiate is observed and maintained by the mirror of His word!

Although God has the plan of a beautiful life for you, it is your choice to have it as well as the extent to which you are beautified. You can choose your beauty status in the kingdom by your devotion to the word. You may be ugly, but you can change it by your choice to stick to the word. The choice is yours. The tool is available, cheap and affordable. Moreover the Holy Spirit the cosmetologist is ready to help.

> *"Likewise the Spirit also helpeth our infirmities: for we know not what we should pray for as we ought: but the Spirit itself maketh intercession for us with groanings which cannot be uttered. And he that searcheth the hearts knoweth what is the mind of the Spirit because he maketh intercession for the saints according to the will of God"* **(Romans 8:26-7).**

Benefits Of Radiating His Beauty

When you radiate His beauty, you attract everything God

attracts. No blessing eludes you. Jesus radiated God and was in favour, both with God and man. The power of beauty works like a charm. Before you step out, each day, charm-up in the dressing room by studying the word and everything you need will be pursuing you. This charm attracts all you need. **(See Song of Solomon 1:16).**

> *Surely goodness and mercy shall follow me all the days of my life: and I will dwell in the house of the LORD forever* **(Psalms 23: 6).**

Beauty gives confidence and control. When you radiate His beauty, you are confident and not afraid; you are bold to approach Him. God's beauty or glory opens doors. David was brought to Saul's palace, because of his godly nature.

Before I conclude this chapter, it is important you understand what God's beauty is, the characteristics.

God's beauty is divine wisdom from above. When you operate it, it makes your face shine. The real state of your face is not the makeup you wear, but the wisdom you operate. There are two kinds of wisdom- heavenly and earthly wisdom.

Heavenly wisdom makes you beautiful, while earthly wisdom makes you ugly. So choose the status of your face by the wisdom you operate. We live in a world where people are crazy about their looks. Everyone wants to look the best any day and everywhere. No one wants to age. People spend so much money on makeup and cosmetics, neglecting the real beauty, which is the unfading beauty of God within you.

If you operate heavenly wisdom, even at eighty years you will still be looking beautiful and attractive. This is the reason Sarah stood out. Sin is anti-beauty and can suddenly make you ugly, so resist it. Carry your beauty with great care. Be careful how and what you say, act well and be guarded by the word. Never do what the word disapproves. And your life will remain beautiful and empowered for the works of righteousness.

CHAPTER 3

Transferring Of Beauty

When you possess beauty; God's blessings and nature; God expects you to transfer it to others. Any beauty that is not transferred will soon diminish and fade. Every goodness and nature of God you possess should be passed on, or it will fizzle and vanish. Do you have His blessing? Pass them on.

Spiritual blessings are also to be passed on.

> *"For I long to see you, that I may impart unto you some spiritual gift, to the end ye may be established; That is, that I may be comforted together with you by the mutual faith both of you and me"* **(Romans1:11-12).**

Comfort others with the comfort you have received from the Lord. The major reason God is blessing you is for others. He is using you as a channel to reach others.

> *"Behold, I will do a new thing; now it shall spring forth; shall ye not know it? I will even make a way in the wilderness,* **and** *rivers in the desert. The beast of the field shall honour me, the dragons and the owls: because I give waters in the wilderness,* **and** *rivers in the desert, to give drink to my people, my chosen"* (Isaiah 43: 19-20).

By transferring of beauty, I mean impacting lives around you with the blessings of God in your life so much that in turn, they will desire your God. Show love to people to the extent they want your God. People do not care what you know or your relationship with God until they know how much you care. When you care for someone, you can win him/her to Christ even without a word. Action speaks louder than words.

Love enables transfer of beauty. Love is the vehicle that transfers God's beauty. It takes love to share what you have with others. When love is in place beauty transfer becomes automatic and easy. Jesus transferred the beauty and nature of God because of compassion. Every miracle and works He did was out of compassion. Until you have love, you cannot transfer beauty.

Who are you expected to pass beauty to? In other words who does God expect you to love? God expects you to do good (transfer beauty) to all especially believers.

> *"As we have therefore opportunity, let us do good unto all* **men**, *especially unto them who are of the household of faith"* (Galatians 6:10).

Therefore, there are two classes of people to do good to and unconditionally to love:

- *The World (Unsaved)*

- *The Believers (Saved)*

Transferring Beauty To The Unsaved:

> *"Ye have heard that it hath been said, Thou shalt love thy neighbour, and hate thine enemy. But I say unto you, Love your enemies, bless them that curse you, do good to them that hate you, and pray for them which despitefully use you, and persecute you; That ye may be the children of your Father which is in heaven: for he maketh his sun to rise on the evil and on the good, and sendeth rain on the just and on the unjust. "For if ye love them which love you, what reward have ye? Do not even the publicans the same? And if ye salute your brethren only, what do ye more* **than others?** *Do not even the publicans so? Be ye therefore perfect, even as your Father which is in heaven is perfect"* **(Matthew 5: 43-48).**

When you reach the unsaved with God's love (loving and caring for them), you win them to God. God's love is a powerful tool for evangelism. No one can resist love, for love conquers all things.

When you reach the unsaved with love, you make God irresistible to them. This is the tool missionaries used to win many souls and brought the light of God to dark regions. When you show people you care, they will care to know that God whom you serve.

Every blessing of God in your life is a potential tool to reach the unsaved. Your job, money, house, cars, talent, skill, etc. are effective evangelism tools, to win others to the Lord Jesus Christ.

When you win the unsaved, through your kindness, you will shine as the brightness of the firmament; that is God will bless you so much that you stand out; standing out in beauty. **(Daniel 12:3)** When you embrace evangelism, your life will be beautified. Find time to care for people, share your food, say a kind word, hand out tracts, etc. and you will be amazed at the blessing God will bring to you.

How beautiful are the feet of those that preach the good news? When your feet are beautiful, it means your whole body is beautiful. You need not to wash the whole body Jesus said if your feet have been washed. If you desire total beauty, then explore evangelism. No wonder he that wins souls is wise. Be wise and generous in using your gifts to increase the kingdom by bringing souls to Christ.

God's miracle in your life is for you to tell others and win them to Christ. The field around you is ripe for harvest. Many are hurting in pain so that you can let your sickle of love to harvest them into the kingdom. Do not close your ears to their cries, nor let your hands hang loose. Put your hands to the plough by your acts of love.

> *"Therefore said he unto them, the harvest truly is great, but the labourers* **are** *few: pray ye, therefore, the Lord of the harvest, that he would send forth labourers into his harvest."* **(Luke 10:2).**

There is no better chance to show love and win people over, than now. When people around you hurt it is a sign they are ripe for harvest, only let down the sickle of your love. Reach out to people in hospitals, prisons, offices, schools, etc. Cease every opportunity to do good peradventure; you may win them to Christ.

> *"Arise, shine; for thy light is come, and the glory of the LORD is risen upon thee. For, behold, the darkness shall cover the earth, and gross darkness the people: but the LORD shall arise upon thee, and his glory shall be seen upon thee."* **(Isaiah 60:1-2)**

When the darkness of pain and loss prevail, shine the light of God's love, and people will be drawn to God. Ensure you leave a person better than you met him because you are a channel of God's blessing and love.

Transferring Beauty To The Saved

The next group you are expected to transfer beauty to is the saved. Love fellow believers, people in your Local Christian assembly and beyond.

> **Galatians 6:10** *"As we have therefore opportunity, let us do good unto all* **men***, especially unto them who are of the household of faith."*

God expects you to do good to them especially. Why does God want you to do good, especially to believers? Because they are of the same household with you and He is your Father as well as theirs. We all belong to Him. People should not be hungry in your house, and you are distributing food outside. Charity begins at home. It is very important to reach out to fellow believers because your fellowship is with the Father and the brethren. When you fellowship with God, extend it to fellow believers, only then is the cycle complete. Extend the blessing you receive from God to them.

You cannot say you love God and fellowship with Him when you do not fellowship or communicate with the brethren. You cannot say you love God if you do not love the brethren you see. Loving one another is so crucial that God made it a commandment, not a suggestion. God commands us to love one another and only by this all men will know we are his disciple.

> *"A new commandment I give unto you, that ye love one another; as I have loved you, that ye also love one another. By this shall all* **men** *know that ye are my disciples if ye have love one to another"* (**John 13: 34-35**).

Before God, the proof of your Christianity is not how much you pray, speak in tongues, preach, or the car you drive, but your love for others. The foundation of Christianity is love. God so love us and gave us Jesus. Jesus loved and gave His life. Abraham loved and gave Isaac his son. The early believers loved and shared all they had in common and non-lacked. If you are a member of God's household, you must love. It is a commandment and not an option. Love is the trademark of Christianity.

Your ability to love and share with others is what makes you a Christian. Christ loved to the extent of giving His life, and that is the extent to which we are required to love one another.

You have not loved to the extent of giving your life, so do not complain yet. How you are identified as a Christian is not by the accumulation of things but in your distribution of them. If love is a commandment, then you must share what you have not just when it is convenient. Jesus taught that if you have two coats share with him, that has none so that your faith will be activated by love to yield abundantly. For faith worketh by love. When your faith is accompanied by love, giving, it procures much more than you gave.

> *"Except a grain of corn falls to the ground, it abides alone, but when it falls and dies, it grows and brings much fruit"* **(John 12:24).**

When you distribute that one beauty of yours, it abounds. This is the principle of Faith working by love. When love is in place, your Faith yields so much.

Do you need dresses or finance? Reach out in love to that brother or sister in need, and you will reap bountifully. Begin to share the little you have, and you will have it back abundantly. Love is a command because God desires your faith to work tremendously for your beauty. Put your faith to work, by your love works. *"For as the body without the spirit is dead, so faith without works is dead also."* **(James 2: 26)** Your love towards the brethren makes your Faith alive to obtain.

The commandment to love one another is not optional but compulsory. You must love and give whether you feel like it or not, whether you like the person or not, whether the recipient is grateful or not. You must love because you are a custodian of God's love, nature, and beauty which must be dispensed to others. When you function in this capacity as a channel of blessing, you will be replenished, even more abundantly. (See **Luke6: 38, Proverbs 11:25, Ecclesiastes 11:1-2**)

The commandment to love is for your good, to maximize in beauty. Every member of Christ body has something to give. Everyone has something to supply to make the body grow.

> *"There is* **one body, and one Spirit, even as ye are called in one hope of your calling"** (Ephesians 4:16).

We all have received grace, according to our gifts. You have something to give; it might not be material; it could be spiritual, a word or prayer. When you see a sister or brother going through a challenge, you can invest your time by praying for her or him. When God blesses you with the revelation of the word, call some people and share it.

A simple word of encouragement does a lot. Use your talent to bless people. If you have a good voice, bless others with your songs. Rejoice with them that rejoice. Mourn with them that mourn. The command to love is to everyone. Do not count yourself out and miss the benefits associated with this command. If you are born again and belong to Christ, you have something to give. This means that you are a candidate of beauty because whatever you give comes back to you. The reward of transferring beauty through love and giving enriches and perfects your beauty.

God will perfect beauty in Zion, the Church, when people reach out to one another in love, supplying what the other lacks. **(Acts 2: 44-45)**

It is my prayer that you will not be weary in well doing, that your love and giving will not go cold. You shall be fervent in loving and giving, and it will be measured back to you.

God will multiply and return to you, whatever seed you sow. Let love be your watchword. Look out for opportunities to be a blessing to others. *"Freely you have received, and freely you should give."* (Matthew 10:8) If God did not withhold it from you, do not withhold it from others. God did not wait for you to qualify for His blessing so let mercy prevail in your giving. The comfort of God in your pains has equipped you to comfort others.

Paul told Timothy to be apt to teach and not neglect the teaching of the word. Whatever beauty you received from the Lord, pass it on. Pass joy on. Pass on that smile. Share your food and shelter. Always remember, for every love you sow, a reward awaits you.

> *And let us not be weary in well doing: for in due season we shall reap if we faint not"* (**Galatians 6:9**).

To what extent does God expect me to love others? To the extent He loves you. If Jesus gave His life for you, what are you willing to give up for others? Loving others helps you maintain and thrive in beauty.

CHAPTER 4

Vision For Beauty

Beauty is God's intent and plan for man. God intends man to live a beautiful life, a life of abundance and blessing. He demonstrated this at creation. Before He created Adam, everything Adam might need was in place, even in abundance. *"And the LORD God planted a garden eastward in Eden, and there he put the man whom he had formed."* **(Genesis 2:8)** That's the beauty God intends for you now in Christ Jesus. **(John 10:10, Ephesians 2:12-13).**

There is a Garden for you here in this life, where all you need to be beautiful is available. Until you are in your garden, you will not fully manifest the beauty God has for you.

What is this Garden? For Adam, the garden was his place of assignment. God put Adam in the garden to tend it. Your garden is the place of God's assignment for you. Discovering

God's assignment for you puts you in your garden, where everything you need is found. Understanding God's assignment (Purpose and Plan) for your life is called Vision.

Vision is defined as insight into God's plan, purpose, and programme for your life. When you discover vision and live by it, you are in your Garden of Eden, exploring the blessings God has made available to you. I want you to know that before you were born an assignment has been waiting for you. In fact, to fulfill that assignment is the reason you were created. Just like Adam was created to till the earth and have dominion over it you are created for a specific assignment.

> *"Before I formed thee in the belly I knew thee, and before thou camest forth out of the womb I sanctified thee, and I ordained thee a prophet unto the nations"* (Jeremiah 1:5).

> *"For we are his workmanship, created in Christ Jesus unto good works, which God hath before ordained that we should walk in them"* (Ephesians 2:10).

When you make Jesus the Lord of your life, He will begin to lead you in the path of your assignment. Jesus told Peter and others.

> *"And he said unto them, Follow me and I will make you fishers of Men."* (Matthew 4:19).

When you follow Jesus by reading His word, prayer and fellowshipping with other believers, He begins to make you who He created you to be. If you do not know, you are being made every time you hear the word of God. The word deposits grace in your life and build you up. It may not be dramatic, but with time you will begin to notice changes in your life.

In this chapter, I will be sharing with you how to discover and live vision. If you desire a vision for your beauty, go to God for it. God is the custodian of visions not man. Set time to be away from the crowd and go to God. Notice, God took Adam to the garden and gave him specific instructions.

> *"I will stand upon my watch, and set me upon the tower, and will watch to see what he will say unto me, and what I shall answer when I am reproved. And the LORD answered me, and said, Write the vision, and make it plain upon tables, that he may run that readeth it. For the vision is yet for an appointed time, but at the end, it shall speak, and not lie: though it tarry, wait for it; because it will surely come, it will not tarry"* (Habakkuk 2:1-3).

Your vision is neither people's choice nor vote. It is not the trend, nor the highest paid job. It is not even men's opinion, but God's.

There is an assignment God has for putting you where you are; discover it.

> *"I will lead and guide you in the path you shall choose"* (Psalms 32:8).

> *"The steps of the righteous are ordered by God"* (Psalms 37:23).

"For I know the thoughts that I think toward you, saith the LORD, thoughts of peace, and not of evil, to give you an expected end" (Jeremiah 29:11).

It does not matter the good thoughts someone has towards you it cannot equate God's thought and plans for you. When you discover vision, you begin to manifest the beauty it is designed to give you.

"How precious also are thy thoughts unto me, O God! how great is the sum of them! If I should count them, they are more in number than the sand: when I awake, I am still with thee" (Psalm 139: 17-18).

"Thou art worthy, O Lord, to receive glory and honour and power: for thou hast created all things, and for thy pleasure, they are and were created" (Revelation 4:11).

This chapter is very important if you must express the beauty of God in you. If you do not discover vision, you will wander in life, famished and ugly. **(Song of Solomon 1:6)** When the disciples abandoned their assignment after Jesus ascended to heaven, they toiled and toiled in vain. This is the major reason people are toiling in life, jobs, and marriages, etc. They failed to discover and follow the vision.

Discovering vision is not optional but mandatory for a beautiful life. Until Jesus discovered vision, no eye was on Him.

"The Spirit of the Lord is upon me, because he hath anointed me to preach the gospel to the poor; he hath sent me to heal the brokenhearted, to preach deliverance to the captives, and recovering of sight to the blind, to set at liberty them that are bruised, to preach the acceptable year of the Lord" (Luke 4:17).

But as soon as He discovered vision, He was beautified, and people were attracted to Him.

Your lack of vision could possibly be the reason it seems you are neglected. When you are on your assignment, providing solution to people's need, they cannot but look up to you. After this chapter, you shall discover your vision and the people that had looked down on you will begin to look up to you. Vision makes you indispensable. Do not take it out on anyone when you are ignored, simply discover vision, and you will be noticed and announced.

STEPS TO DISCOVERING VISION

1. Set Time Alone With God

Leave the crowd to hear the voice of God. If you stay with the crowd, you will be led by it and miss your purpose. No one that follows the crowd leads the crowd.

"Through desire a man, having separated himself, seeketh and intermeddleth with all wisdom." (Prov. 18:1)

When you are away from the noise, you will hear God for direction. Please separate to gain insight into what God wants you to do and be positioned for your beauty.

2. Praise And Worship Him

When you praise and worship God speaks.

> *Ye shall have a song, as in the night when a holy solemnity is kept; and gladness of heart, as when one goeth with a pipe to come into the mountain of the LORD, to the mighty One of Israel. And the LORD shall cause his glorious voice to be heard, and shall shew the lighting down of his arm, with the indignation of his anger, and with the flame of a devouring fire, with scattering, and tempest, and hailstones"* **(Isaiah 30:29-30).**

3. Be Sensitive, Watch And See What He Shall Say To You

> *"My sheep hear my voice, and I know them, and they follow me. I give them eternal life, and they will never perish, and no one will snatch them out of my hand"* (John 10:27-28).

> *"And he said to them, "Pay attention to what you hear: with the measure you use, it will be measured to you, and still more will be added to you"* (Mark 4:24).

MEANS GOD USES TO RELEASE VISION

When you set out time to discover vision God communicates to you. God could reveal vision through some of these means.

1. His Word

The word of God is the manual for everyone He created. Is God your creator? If yes, then your life has a bearing on His word. It is your responsibility to discover it. **(Psalm 40:7, Luke 4:17).** There should be specific scripture that your life is fashioned along; a scripture in which your life revolves.

Mine is **Isaiah 61:3:**

> *"To appoint unto them that mourn in Zion, to give unto them beauty for ashes, the oil of joy for mourning, the garment of praise for the spirit of heaviness; that they might be called trees of righteousness, the planting of the LORD, that he might be glorified."*

As you wait on God, be sensitive He will direct you to a place in the Bible that has your assignment. The particular scripture will describe your assignment. Until you discover it, the house of your life is not built and much less beautified. When you discover this scripture and live by it, it creates all you need and repels every darkness around you. The word is most authentic way visions are discovered.

2. Dreams

Joseph discovered vision through dreams. Do you dream where you are preaching to a crowd? That could be a pointer to your purpose. Note that any dream that is contrary to God's word is not vision.

3. Desire

After you have prayed, God might put a strong desire in you to do something. That could be an indication of your vision.

4. Opportunity

Vision could come to you as opportunities. So seize it. Isaiah's vision came as an opportunity *"Who shall I send and who we will go for us."* **(Isaiah 6:8)** David stepped into his vision through opportunity.

5. Godly Counsel

God might pass vision to you through Godly counsellors; most times it confirms what you already knew. Otherwise, seek confirmation from God. Do not jump into something because someone said so. Seek God's confirmation and until you have His backing, do not move. Elizabeth counselled Mary on her divine assignment as a confirmation of the message she had received earlier from Angel Gabriel.

> *"Thy way is in the sea, and thy path in the great waters and thy footsteps are not known. Thou leddest thy people like a flock by the hand of Moses and Aaron"* **(Palms 77: 19-20).**

6. Burden

God might place a burden on you as your vision. Nehemiah's vision to rebuild the wall of Jerusalem came as a burden.

Whichever way your vision comes it must be clear and precise. It must agree with the word of God and demonstrate God's love to humanity. God will never give you an assignment that is contrary to His word and ways. Every vision carries peace and grace to perform.

When God releases vision, write it down so you will not forget it. It is so important because your life depends on it. (Hebrew 4:1) Every detail of your assignment has particular beauty it is designed to add to you.

Living Vision Or Running With Vision

Habakkuk 2:2 says;

"Write the vision that he that reads may run."

After you have written your vision, you are expected to run with it; effect it. Visions are to be implemented. Any vision that is not lived out is useless and procures no beauty.

After God took Adam to the garden, Adam tended the garden. He was on his assignment. Visions are not just to be celebrated, advertised but implemented. Until you implement your vision you will not get the blessing God has for you. Until you labour in your vision, you are not rewarded.

"But without faith, it is impossible to please him: for he that cometh to God must believe that he is and that he is a rewarder of them that diligently seek him" **(Hebrew11:6).**

God only rewards diligent labourers.

Visions are not lived recklessly but diligently. I assure you if your assignment is from God you need hard work to accomplish it. God is big, and He gives big assignments.

You Need The Following To Run With Your Vision

Diligence

> *"Whatever your hand finds to do, do it with your might; for there is no work or device or knowledge or wisdom in the grave where you are going"* (Ecclesiastes 9:10).

Focus

This is one thing that is needed in your life, for your assignment, so focus on it. If your eye is singled on your assignment, your whole body will be full of light. When you have discovered your assignment, do not turn to the left or right, make a straight path for yourself. You cannot be busy with so many things and excel in your assignment.

Passion

Be in love with your assignment and be willing to sacrifice for it. Anything you do not love you will not stay long with it. If your assignment is lifelong, I tell you that you should be passionate enough to live by it. Nothing gives me greater joy than what I am doing now. What you are not willing to do without pay is not your vision. And anything you have to do only because of money is not your vision. No sacrifice is too much for me to make for my vision.

Patience

No one understands patience more than a farmer or gardener. Crops do not grow the next day after you planted them. They need patient watering and nurturing to grow and produce, so it is with vision. Patience is needed to run the race of vision

"Wherefore seeing we also are compassed about with so great a cloud of witnesses, let us lay aside every weight and the sin which doth so easily beset us, and let us run with patience the race that is set before us" (Hebrew 12:1).

God has a timetable for your assignment, and it has to be done that way. You need the patience to go by God's timetable.

Faith

After God brought Adam to the garden, He spoke to Him and gave Him instructions. What God spoke to Adam produced faith needed to run vision. If you must run with vision, you need faith to do what God says, even when it makes no sense. Your assignment is from God who you do not see, so faith must be in place to relate to Him. If you must succeed in your assignment, the word of God must have a prominent place in life. **(See Josh 1:8, 2Timothy 3:15-16).**

The word builds you; gives you life, strength, joy, grace and all you need to do the assignment. The word also charts the path.

A man of vision must not trade his word time for anything. God's word should be very important in your life.

Positive Confession

Not only is God's word important, your word (what you say) is also important to the fulfillment of your vision. As a man in authority, your word counts and God approves it. Therefore only speak what you desire for your life. Whatever Adam called anything in His garden; that was the name. God did not change it because that was Adam's domain and choice. Be careful and thoughtful of what you say about your vision. And also be careful of what you say about your children, husband, wife, friends or anything you have influence over for you shall reap it.

Words are like seeds, when spoken they are sown and grow in your garden. Only speak what you desire and want to see. Remember your garden is watered and fertile and would produce any seed sown in it. Be careful. Beautify your garden by your carefully chosen words.

Trusting And Resting In The Lord

Until Adam slept, God could not bring Eve. In the pursuit of your vision, have confidence in God to provide your needs. Rest in the confident assurance that God will never leave, nor forsake you as He has promised in the word.

> *"Be strong and of a good courage, fear not, nor be afraid of them: for the LORD thy God, it is he that doth go with thee; he will not fail thee, nor forsake thee"* **(Deuteronomy 31:6).**

If it is an assignment from Him, He will provide for it. God of the vision is God of the provision. Pro-Vision means God has provided before the vision. That means all you might need for the execution of your vision has already been fully provided.

My prayer is that God will open your eyes and lead you to them per time. Do not fret or you will be too drained to tend the garden He has assigned you.

Gratitude

Adam showed profound gratitude when God brought Eve.

> *"This is the bone of my bone and flesh of my flesh"* **(Genesis 2:23).**

In that same way express profound gratitude to God for every provision and cherish it. Listen, whenever God brings people to help you in your vision appreciate and cherish them. Do not boss them around or treat them as less important. They are not working for you but working with you. Because they also are fulfilling their assignment from God and together God's purpose is accomplished by all. They are your destiny helpers. Accomplishments in life are products of the good relationships God brings to you. Honour people, treat them respectfully and they will afford you the help God designed. Anything you are grateful for and treat with respect will keep abounding.

Good Company

Although relationship, in general, is important; but not everyone is helpful for your vision. Wisdom demands you identify the right relationship and adapt accordingly. When you stay with the wise, you become wiser, but companies of fools shall be destroyed.

"Do not be deceived evil communication corrupts good morals" **(1 Corinthians 15:33).**

"Blessed is the man that walks not in the counsel of the ungodly nor sit in the seat of the scornful" **(Psalms 1:1).**

Examine each relationship, does it take you closer to your destiny or pull you away from it? Any friend that does not encourage you to be who God wants you to be is not good for you. He will rob you of your beauty. In your life, there are friends you necessarily must detach from for your beauty.

Friendship is by choice not by force. You owe no man so do not be afraid to detach. It is your destiny we are talking about.

If your peer group influence is negative, detach from them. Any group you cannot freely talk about God is unsafe for you. And any friend you cannot discuss the bible with is not for you. Let your love for God and His word determine your relationship. Relate to people of the same mind and passion towards God and His kingdom. And this should also determine who you marry.

A man of vision is not tied to any relationship or family. The man that desired to follow Jesus in (Luke 9: 61-62) said;

"I will follow you, Lord, but first let me go and say goodbye to my family" Jesus replied, "No one who puts his hand to the plough and looking back is fit for the kingdom of God."

Jesus said that His family; mother, father and brethren are those that hear the word of God and do them. These were people of like mind. Do not be eternally bound to any relationship or you miss your purpose.

> *"Be ye not unequally yoked together with unbelievers: for what fellowship hath righteousness with unrighteousness? and what communion hath light with darkness?"* (2 Cor. 6:14).

Humility

In your pursuit of vision be humble enough to be open and transparent. Be humble enough to be "Naked." Do not claim and behave like you know everything. When you make a mistake admit it. If you are not humble, you will not receive help from God or people. When you are "Naked" (humble), you are approachable, and people can clothe you with their beauty (offer you help).

The fact that God has ordained you for that vision does not mean you know everything and can do it independently. You need helpers. And nothing attracts helpers than humility.

Apollos was humble enough to take help from Aquila and Priscilla (Acts 18) and that enhanced His beauty. Give room for people to impact and clothe you which enhances your beauty. Seek advice and help from proven people. Do not pretend to be who you are not, be yourself.

Rest

God rested on the seventh day not because He needed to rest but to demonstrate the importance of rest. As a visionary, rest is mandatory, not optional, especially after a demanding task. Take good rest in between tasks.

Jesus several times retreated from His disciples and got the benefits of the seventh day. God blessed the seventh day, the day of rest. That means there are blessing deposited on the seventh day. When you take a good rest, you enjoy the blessings of the seventh day. You come out refreshed empowered to continue with vision. Moreover, you gain inspiration and fresh revelation to move the work on.

Your body works and needs to rest to carry your spirit to the end of your earthly life. Vision is lifelong; if you do not take rest, you will be laid to rest faster. When you are tired, pamper yourself, spoil yourself, take a vacation, do things you love to do outside your vision. It must not be work all the time and every day. When your body complains, take time to recreate. Good sleep, good hotels, and a healthy menu, music, exercise, swim, are some ways to recreate.

Recently I did not realize how much I needed rest until I travelled to Chicago to visit my niece. It was refreshing and recreating, being away from home; from the cries of my two-year-old and the demands of my teenagers. I came back a different person; overwhelmed by God's presence and grace.

Sometimes, take time out to be alone with God. Do not be engrossed in activities and forget to take care of yourself. Caring for others and not having time for yourself is not healthy in the long run. Your body needs to rest to carry your Spirit long enough to complete the assignment. If you die for lack of rest, God will hold you accountable for the unfinished work. So be wise.

Confidence

Like Adam, you have been equipped to do your assignment by the word and Spirit of God. Do not be afraid; you have what it takes. God's Spirit is expressed through you as grace (God's working ability) which shows as your gift.

When you discover your gift; what you do with ease, nurture it, groom it for your effectiveness in vision. Your gift is what you trade for your beauty. The five–talent man in the Bible traded with his talents and got an extra five talents. The more you use your talent, the more your beauty shines. For example, because I am using my writing talent, I have gone from one book to many books. As I use it more often, I increase the output for more beauty. Yield your talent to the Holy Spirit.

Do What He Says

As you imbibe these nuggets, you shall excel in your vision.

My Beautiful Life

CHAPTER 5

Marital Beauty

God is not just interested in His assignment for you; He is interested in your marriage as well and who you marry. God desires a good marriage for everyone that is why His word is given to help in the choice of who you marry. God brought Eve to Adam, gave Adam Eve, and gave Eve Adam. Marital destiny is very important because it affects every area of your life. When your marriage is shaky, you are unstable in every area of your life especially your assignment in the kingdom.

If you desire to realize your marriage destiny, the word of God should lead you to the right choice.

> *"This book of the law shall not depart out of thy mouth; but thou shalt meditate therein day and night, that thou mayest observe to do according to all that is written therein: for then*

thou shalt make thy way prosperous, and then thou shalt have good success" (Joshua 1:8).

"House and riches may come from the father, but a prudent wife comes from God" (Proverbs 19:14).

"He that finds a wife finds a good thing and obtains favour from God" (Proverbs 18:22).

God honours your search for a wife or husband so search for a good one by His word and spirit. Who you marry should not be determined by money, status, skin colour, race, tribe, but by God; His word and Spirit.

Parents should trust God to help their children make the right choices of marriage. Your responsibility as a parent is to lead them to Christ, teach them the word and trust God to lead them. Many parents, because of fear have led their Children into wrong marriages that have marred their beauty. Nothing makes you ugly like a wrong marriage. Trust God to lead your children into good marriages by His word and Spirit.

If you are single, do not allow anyone to pressurize you into making a wrong or untimely choice. When you make a godly choice in marriage, you are decorated with extra beauty. You are decorated with the honour God has designed marriage for. *"Marriage is honourable in all things"* (Hebrews 13:4).

Honour enhances beauty. As a woman, there is a man God has equipped whose assignment will enhance yours for beauty.

Allow God by His word to take you to him. Never condone any relationship that God's word disapproves. You can begin now to pray for him so that when he shows up, you will recognize him. If you marry the wrong person, you will not be needed, valued nor appreciated because you are in the wrong place.

God brought the woman He created to the man. Marriage is between man and woman, not for boys and girls. So, girl, you got no business with any man or boy until you are ready to marry and help. That is why boyfriend and girlfriend stuff is not a God thing and simply condemned by the word. Age and maturity have a major role in marriage. You must be old enough mentally and physically mature to marry. God took the woman to the man, not the girl to the boy. God is not part of boy and girl sexual relationship or live-in.

If God is not in that relationship, definitely the devil is, through lust. That is why the divorce rate is so high because girls and boys marry to break. When a marriage is between girl and boy, they will compound each other's problem rather than help. She will get pregnant and drop out of school or drop in her grade. They bring misery to each other. Girl, you have no business with any man or boy until you are made by God and mature by His word. Then you are set to render help to your husband.

You have to be mature and afford help to yourself first, before helping another person. Come out of that illicit relationship and be where God can make you into what He wants. Be in school, church, and other good places. And when He is done making you, He will take you to your man.

Boy, you do not need any help until you are a man, built by God and have identified and involved with your assignment. Eve was brought to Adam to help with His assignment. You should first of all be man enough to provide for her. Boys and girls do not joggle up your life or let anyone do that to you. There is time to be made, and there is time to help others.

Teenage is time to be made. If you help at the time you should be made, you are drained, crushed, destroyed, frustrated and give up. Life should be fun if you understand that God has made all things beautiful in its time and follow it. Beauty is added to you when you marry at the right time.

You will be grounded if you carry someone when you could barely walk. Both of you will fall woefully, disgracefully and painfully. Your marital destiny is bright do not mar it with unnecessary relationships.

> *"To everything, there* **is** *a season and a time to every purpose under the heaven"* (Ecclesiastes 3:1).

I shatter every chain that the devil has used to keep you in that wrong relationship. I break every ungodly and untimely soul tie. You are set free to run with your destiny. I deliver you from every snare of the Evil One. You are contacting the anointing that breaks every yoke right now. As heaven's representative, I stamp heaven's disapproval to that ungodly relationship. Heaven will scatter you, and the earth shall no longer condone you. I release the angel of God to separate you and keep you safe until your time comes. It is done. You are free to pursue your vision. Congratulations!

Your marital destiny is preserved. The anointing of God from this book shall keep you unspotted from the world and sin. God has sanctified you to Himself. There is nothing that weighs down and destroys a young girl than premarital sexual relationships. It gives her responsibility when she is too young and which she is unsuitable for. Her young soul is overwhelmed and weighed down making her look older than her age, tarnishing her beauty. At fourteen she will look thirty-six. Before twenty-five, she is already a grandma. Oh my God, what a pitiable life!

Girl, preserve your beauty by your godly choice; wait for your time. *"God makes everything beautiful in its time...."* (**Ecclesiastes 3:11**) When it is time to marry, and you are in a healthy relationship you are beautified. You are dignified and honourable at the right time. You are only dignified and beautiful, with the opposite-sex relationship at the right time, outside that you are indeed ugly. Do not turn a thing of beauty to shame, wait for your time.

Marriage is honourable; adds honour to you, when the bed is undefiled. Sex outside marriage defiles the bed and brings shame and reproach to your beauty. So stop it. Pregnancy outside marriage is shame and reproach, no matter its prevalence and acceptance in the modern society. Because something is common and politically correct does not mean it is right or Godly. Premarital sex is eternally ugly.

Stop that premarital or extramarital sexual relationship so that God's beauty will be perfected in you. It does not matter who you are or who you are with, premarital and extramarital sex corrodes your beauty. **(Read Prov.6: 26-29).**

After this chapter, you will be empowered to say no and stay unspotted in this perverse world.

> *"Wherewithal shall a young man cleanse his way? by taking heed thereto according to thy word"* **(Psalm 119:9).**

It does not matter how dirty or corrupted you have become; the word can cleanse you. It can cleanse your conscience from dead works to serve the living God. Run for your life. Most problems in marriages are from boys and girls living together in the name of marriage due to unplanned pregnancy from premarital sex.

These problems arise from the girl's inability to offer help, and even if she does, the boy is immature to appreciate or accept it. I had struggled with trying to help my two-year-old boy wear his winter jacket during cold days. When I tried to help, he would scream "no mummy I do not want my jacket." I am sure that's not the kind of marriage you desire. A marriage where your sacrifices are not appreciated, neither needed or valued. So refuse premarital sex and relationships. It destroys the foundation of your life.

After God created marriage everything he made was good. In others words, with wrong marriage, everything in your life can become very bad. Choose one. I advise you to wait patiently for God to make and take you to your man. When your parents are protecting you from the opposite sex, it is for your good; do not fight them. Your school stuff alone is enough; you do not need an extra burden. Your heart is too tender to cope with relationship stress and academics at the same time.

Note:

God brought a woman to a man. He did not bring man to man or woman to a woman nor did He bring a man to cat or dog nor woman to a cat or dog. If it is marriage, it must be a man and a woman. Otherwise, it is not marriage. Anything else that people call marriage is not godly; if it does not align with God's standard in the Bible, or does not involve God, then God is not in it. Homosexuality is unacceptable to God and God is not in it. Since God is not in them, the partners involved are opening themselves to satanic attack and destruction. Such practices are devil's scheme to exchange the honour that is yours for shame, pain, and death.

"The devil has come to steal, kill and destroy" (John 10:10).

Run for your life. Flee from those kinds of so-called "Marriages"; they are not marriages. They are concocted traps of the devil for your destruction. God loves you and cares about your soul. Receive power to release you from every satanic trap in Jesus mighty Name. Amen

CHAPTER 6

Creating Your Beauty
(Power Of Spoken Word)

A s soon as God speaks it is established, it does not matter what you think

> *"So shall my word be that goeth forth out of my mouth: it shall not return unto me void, but it shall accomplish that which I please, and it shall prosper in the thing whereto I sent it"* (Isaiah 55:11).

God says your life is beautiful, it is already done.

> *"According as his divine power hath given unto us all things that pertain unto life and godliness, through the knowledge of him that hath called us to glory and virtue"* (2Peter 1:3).

Your beautiful life has already been accomplished. Jesus finished it on the cross. He died that the blessings of Abraham might flow to you for beauty. Once God says it, it is created in the heavens. God has done His part, and it is now left for you to do your part. You have a role to play in manifesting your beautiful life that He has created.

Every blessing you desire that makes God solely responsible is a fake one and not faith. You are a collaborator with God for your beauty. God expects you to be involved in the physical creation of your beauty. Your cooperation indicates your choice. God cannot force anything on you. Of all that God created, man is the only one with the privilege of choice. And your choice is very important to your blessings.

> *I call heaven and earth to record this day against you, that I have set before you life and death, blessing and cursing: therefore, choose life, that both thou and thy seed may live"* **(Deuteronomy 30:19).**

That something is an obvious need does not make it automatic for God to respond. Jesus asked the Blind man *"What do you want me to do for you"* **(Mark 10:51).** To Jesus, the fact that the man was blind was no indication that he wanted to be healed. Some blind men may need money than the opening of their eyes. Your choice is an important step to experiencing your beautiful life.

If a beautiful life is your choice, I will teach you in this chapter what to do to authenticate and express your choice.

The validation of your choice is your word. What makes me know what you choose is your word. God has made your life beautiful, your marriage, academics, job, and children, beautiful, but you must choose them by your words. As you speak the right words, you give life to your choice. Right confession is very important if your life is to be beautiful. One of the roles you are expected to live by for your beautiful life is Right Confession.

Exploring The Power Of Confession

God

From Genesis, we saw how God turned the earth that was without form and void into a beautiful one. God did not cry nor give up. He spoke what He wanted, and they came to pass. His spoken words made the earth very beautiful.

> *"And God saw everything that he had made, and, behold, it was very good. And the evening and the morning were the sixth day."* (Genesis 1: 31)

God created the beauty He desired by His words. The Earth was beautiful to the extent God spoke; this is the power of positive confession, the spoken word.

Your life is depending on your words to be beautiful. Do not close your mouth, speak what you desire and sooner or later it shall come to pass. **(Proverbs 18:20-21)** Open your mouth wide, and God will fill your life with the blessings you desire. God spoke light prior to other things. No matter the challenges and darkness you are presently facing, with the light of God's word, you shall be beautified.

When Satan comes to mar your beauty, hold firm to the light of God's word and speak what the word says and you will become out beautiful. Will, there be challenges in your life, to mar your beauty? I say a big yes, but you can get Satan running and repel every darkness by the light of God's word. Evil and the evil ones cannot be established in the atmosphere of the word and light. They hate the light because their deeds are evil. Until there is darkness; wordlessness, the devil cannot mar your beauty. Have you noticed that things go wrong if you do not study the word?

Another Good Example Is Paul And Silas

Paul and Silas were bound in the prison, wounded and in pain, and rather than complain, they sang praises to God, and God intervened. There is so much power in what you say about your life and everyone in your world. This is the reason God changed Abram to Abraham, Sarai to Sarah, and Peter to Cephas. God called Gideon the mighty man of valour. He told Jeremiah *"Say not I am a child"* (**Jeremiah 1:7).**

When you are challenged know that you are not alone, God is with you by the word He has spoken. And His spirit is brooding over that situation. All you need to do is to get the light of the word and speak it and create your beautiful life.

In your affliction, He (God) is afflicted. He will never leave you nor forsake you. Many people lose beauty at times of challenge, but your case can be different if you stick to the word and confess it.

How Do The Words I Speak Create My Beauty?

Words have creative abilities to create (John 1:3, Hebrew 11:3) Words are spirits, they are seeds and life. Being spirits, they transcend into the spirit realm and reproduce, causing things to happen in the natural world. God created the world by the power in His word and upholds all things by the same word. Not only does God's word you speak produce your beauty, but it also upholds it. God has given you a mouth and wisdom which none of your adversaries can gainsay nor resist.

> *"For I will give you a mouth and wisdom, which all your adversaries shall not be able to gainsay nor resist"* **(Luke 21:15).**

It does not matter how strong your adversaries are; they cannot resist your word. God's words that you speak are powerful and quick. This is why you should be careful what you say. Do not say before an angel it was a mistake because they hearken to the word. Your words are like orders to the angels to perform. Angels are ministering spirits to you, so they obey your word. Angels take your words as a command, so no matter how bad your situation is, speak the right words. Since angels excel in might, they will execute them. Not only do angels obey your words, but God honours your words also.

"Say unto them, as truly as I live, saith the LORD, as ye have spoken in mine ears, so will I do to you" **(Numbers 14:28).**

Your words are the raw material that God uses to work on your behalf. God is helpless to beautify you if your confession is wrong and contrary to His words. "Whatsoever Adam calls a thing that was the name thereof." God cannot do for you beyond your confession. What do you want God to do for you? Begin to speak it in spite of your challenges.

God magnifies His word above His names," *.... for thou hast magnified thy word above all thy name."* **(Psalm 138:2).** He highly esteems His word, and He expects you to do the same. That is why you shall give an account of every word you speak. No matter your name, status, condition, location, experience, etc. let your words be higher than it. When your word is higher, very soon you will be up and out of the situation. Your words chart the course for you out of every pit. When you speak your name, your situation, status, and condition you remain at the same level.

Could it be that you are at the same level of experience in your health, relationship, career because you say it as it is; establishing the status quo by your words? God told Jeremiah "Say not I am a child." When your experience and condition is contrary to God's plan for you, refuse to identify it by your words, say what you want.

"Say to the righteous it shall be well with him." **(Isaiah 3:10).**

John the Baptist had a voice in the wilderness. Do not allow any wilderness to drown your voice. Let your voice be high, and you will come out of every wilderness. **(Proverbs 12:8, Proverbs 21:23, Proverbs 15:4, James 1:26)**

Your Christianity does not profit you beyond your words because your faith cannot work beyond your confession. When you learn to speak above your circumstance, you will become master of your life, because you are in control, determining the direction of your life. The tongue is like a rudder that directs the ship. When your tongue gets out of control; saying anything your life goes any direction.

Jesus in the midst of storm *spoke* ***"Peace, be still"*** **(Mark 4:39)** and the sea was quiet. When He was told Lazarus was dead; He replied: "He is not dead, but asleep." Towards His crucifixion, He said crucify this body, and on the third day, it shall arise. I believe it was the right Words He spoke at these different hopeless situations that brought positive turns around.

> *"Life and death are in the power of the tongue and he that loves it shall eat the fruits thereof"* **(Proverbs 18:21)**.

This means that your tongue has the power to make something alive or dead. Use it to bring to death to what you want dead, and life to what you want alive.

A good man is satisfied by the increase of his lips, so keep speaking the good things you desire, and they will keep increasing until you are satisfied. Do not keep your mouth closed. Speak out the good things you need and desire. If you desire finances, speak it out and very soon you shall be satisfied with it. Your words are seeds that when planted (spoken) produce your beautiful life. Only be patient and continue speaking and watering it. When a farmer sows His seed, he waters it and patiently waits for it to produce, never giving up.

When God created Adam, He gave him seeds to sow for his provision. Life is all about seed sowing and harvest. Life in itself is the product of seed; the product of your word. So choose the seeds you sow; the words you speak for they will definitely get back to you. Cast your seed upon waters for you will find them after many days; that is, speak what you want in spite of your challenges, and you will have it after many days. It may take many days, but your words have the ability to turn your situations around.

> *"He that observeth the wind shall not sow; and he that regardeth the clouds shall not reap"* **(Ecclesiastes 11:4).**

Your words are seeds that yield the harvest of your life. Reflect, and you will discover that your life today is a product of your words spoken in the past. If you want a better tomorrow, begin to create it today by your spoken words. Speak into your future, sow precious seeds that you will harvest when you get there. Your life cannot be more beautiful than your words. Think about this.

Begin to speak what you desire. I am not saying you will have it right away, but you can begin to sow it and have it later. If you regard the wind (contrary situation) you will not sow, speak the right words. And if you wait for the wind to cease and the situation to be better, it might be too late. This is why the righteous should say "I am healed" "I am highly favoured" and such positive statements have creative powers embedded in them.

Never expound nor give voice to what the enemy is doing in your life for it will multiply and expand. When words multiply they prevail. Take side with God and say your life is beautiful, your family is blessed, your marriage is happy, your business prosperous, and your children are mighty in the land. Use your tongue **wisely** to beautify your life.

> *"A man will be commended according to his wisdom, But he who is of a perverse heart will be despised"* **(Proverbs 12:8).**

Be wise about what you say like a farmer is wise in choosing the kind of seed he plants. If you speak positive words today and negative words tomorrow, the negative words will cancel the effects of the positive words. Negative words set on fire the harvest of the good words you spoke. The effect is that your life goes up and down, and you remain in one stagnant position.

> *"The tongue of the wise is health"* **(Proverbs 12:18).**

Chart a progressive course for your life by your word for you are expected to shine brighter and brighter unto the perfect day. Life and death are in the power of the tongue; you can cause things to live or die in your life by your words. Use its power wisely. You have the power to nullify every work of the enemy in your life. If you cannot say the right word keep quiet. God told Jeremiah, *"Say not I am a child"* (Jeremiah 1:7).

When the situation is compelling you to say something contrary to God's plan and destiny for your life, refuse to speak, or it will mar your beauty. The bad situation may be obvious, but refuse to confess that, or you are empowering it to live. Do not confess anything contrary to God's destiny, purpose, and beauty for your life. The facts may be there, but nothing is true than the word of God. You may be old and sickly but never say so. There is no humility confessing anything that is below what the word of God says about you.

Open your mouth and declare whatsoever you discover from the word about you, it does not matter who is offended. Never accept from anyone anything that is below what God's word says about you. Believe all that God says about you in His word. Never say you can't because the word says you can do all things through Christ. Change your negative confessions about your wife, husband, children, job, colleagues, city, country, etc. When your confession is positive, power is released to bring your expectations to pass.

> *"Behold, I give unto you power to tread on serpents and scorpions, and over all the power of the enemy: and nothing shall by any means hurt you"* **(Luke 10:19).**

Nothing ever gets better with negative words or complaining. That is why God uses positive words. When the adulterous woman was brought to Jesus, He did not condemn her but told her to go and sin no more (John 8:11). God addresses us the Church even in her imperfect state as saints, beloved, sanctified, elects, etc. Does it mean that God does not see her imperfection? No. God sees but chooses to focus on what He wants her to be. The names He calls her bring the change He desires.

I had wondered what He saw in me that He called me into the ministry. He did not call me because I am good enough but He called me with the hope to bring about the change He desired by His word. **(2 Timothy 3:16-17).** As I study and share His word, I am impacted and transformed.

Begin to speak positive words to those in your world, around you and get the beauty they have to offer you. Nothing encourages and brings out the best in someone than positive words. When you are angry and tempted to speak negative words to those around you resist it. The virtuous woman I believe did so much by the power of praise from those in her life.

> *"Many daughters have done virtuously, but thou excellest them all. Favour is deceitful, and beauty is vain: but a woman that feareth the LORD, she shall be praised."* **(Proverbs 31:28-29).**

Many women that would have done as much or even better than the virtuous woman have been stifled due to lack of praise. Who says that the virtuous woman was perfect? But those in her world chose to praise her, and that empowered her to be her best. If you are a child that desires the best from your mum begin to praise her. Every meal I make, I do with conscientiousness, because of the power of praise from my girls. Definitely, I am not the world's best cook, but I am doing my best for them because of their praise.

Praise empowers everyone to be their best. I am up and preaching today, even much better and stronger, against every challenge, because of the praise I get from my team. And that is to their advantage because they are blessed even more. Do not keep your mouth shut, open it wide, let your praise run and beautify your life and those of others. When something is wrong in your life, relationship or job, speak what it should be. "I love you my wife" "I love you my husband" by these, you are instilling strength for the change you desire.

God told me that the changes I desire in my life and anyone else, lies dormant in us, so I should call them forth by my words. You can affect any change or beauty you desire in you and in others by your words. If it is too big for your mouth, it is too big for you. "I say to me, you are blessed and favoured, lacking nothing. My God is supplying all my needs by Christ Jesus. I am divinely lifted above any form of reproach, and the calling and purpose of God in my life is flourishing and blossoming".

Kenneth Copeland's freedom from debt and poverty came through this way. From this story, when he learnt that life was a product of words, he decided to chart a course out of poverty by his words. He confessed God's word of abundance for twelve months, at first nothing happened except that the situation grew worse. He held on, and after twelve months he was completely freed from every debt and had enough to give out. Today he is debt free, prosperous and fulfilled, a blessing to many globally.

This principle works. Lay hold on it and do not give up. Choose to speak the positive things in you and others; do not speak the negatives. If it is too big for your mouth to say positive things about your children, then wonderful kids are out of reach for you. No one can be beyond your confession. Use your words wisely independent of their behaviour and eat the good thereof.

> *"Life and death are in the power of the tongue, and those who love of it shall eat the fruits thereof."* **(Proverbs 18:21)**

The Bible tells us in Deuteronomy 30:19 that,

> *"I have set before you this day good and evil, blessing and cursing, choose good that you may live, choose by your words."*

What you say is what you have chosen. Finally, before we end this chapter, the centurion replied:

> *"I am a man under authority, I say to one do this and he does it, and the other do this, and he does it"* **(Matthew 8:9).**

In the same vein, you redeemed child of God is a man or woman in authority. Jesus has redeemed you Priest and Kings to our God and you reign with your words. That is, you can have it as you desire by your words. For where the word of a King is there is an authority, and no one can stop it. You are in authority, and your words count.

Your words have power. No one can stop it. You can have whatsoever you say. So choose what you wish from life, circumstances, and people by your word. Choose your beauty status in the Kingdom by what you say. Do not speak unwisely; watch out for impatience, anger, and pain for they affect the impact of what you say.

Remember though the tongue is small, it can set the whole body on fire. **(James 3:6).** Be careful, God is at work in your life, ministry, health, marriage, job, etc. Do not be provoked to speak negatively and destroy all the good work He is doing. When you are fixing a relationship, it is destructive to keep talking about past hurts, injuries, and pains. God is not joking when He said *"Forget the former things and consider not the things of the things of old, behold I am about to do a new thing can't you see it"* (Isaiah 43:18-19)

Rehearsing past pain does more damage than good. Choose to see the new thing God is doing from the light of His word and speak them into existence. If you refuse to forget old things, you will not see the new things, because there is no way you can be looking front and back at the same time and expect to make reasonable progress. Do you want a new blessing in that relationship? Forget the past and fix your gaze on the new. If you keep repeating the past mistakes and pain, you remain in a vicious circle. Do you want to break that circle and take your relationship to the next phase; forget the former things! I do not care how justified you may feel to revisit that issues, you cannot be wiser than God. Has blaming and complaining helped you in any way in the past? Then stop it.

You can change your season of life by acting in faith; believing and confessing what the word says. Are you tired of that rocky relationship with God? Try the faith inspired relationship with the Father and all the seasons of dryness and nonproductivity will change. You are the one that determines your season by your words. Confess right and enjoy a good season. Word up to go up. Fill your heart with the word of God, *"....because out of the abundance of the heart the mouth speaks."* (Matthew 12:34). You cannot speak outside what is in your heart. When you have so much of God's word in you, you speak the word and go up.

If you desire change in your life, relationship, job, health, etc. start reprogramming your heart by the word. As you study the word, pains and hurts are replaced by the word. This is called heart reprogramming or mind renewal. You cannot read three verses a day or a few lines of a devotional only and expect a change in your life and relationship. The word must dwell richly in you. If you desire beauty, your priority should be to have word abundantly in your heart for the right confession. You can embark on reading four to five bible chapters daily, or even ten chapters and your life will be transformed before your eyes. Do not live a day without the word or your tank will be low. Guard your hearts with all diligence for out of it are issues of life.

> *"Keep thy heart with all diligence; for out of it are the issues of life"* **(Proverbs 4:23).**

Word up and go up **(Psalms 1:1-4.)** You are not ordinary; you are the righteousness of God in Christ Jesus. And unto you, the righteous light appears in darkness. Redemption gives you access to light which makes you indestructible. Light comes to repel every darkness, so give expression to the light by your words, confess light and not darkness.

God has a word for every challenge you may have. Search it out and begin to confess it and very soon you will be out of that challenge. It is your choice to lighten that bad relationship, ministry, parenthood, etc. You have compassed that mountain enough, turn northwards by your confession. Your tongue is like the rudder of a ship, use it to direct your life well. Until I decided to look at the new thing God is doing in my marriage, I was stuck in same old experience. By your words, you are justified or condemned. Before you leave this chapter note these scriptures that talk about the power of the tongue: **James 1:26, James 3:5-8, Proverbs 12:8, Proverbs 15:4, Proverbs 25:15, and Isaiah 30:37.**

In summary, I leave you with these nuggets.

Do not say it how you feel it, but say what God's word says about it. Be the master of your feelings.

Just as the morning sun renders unimportant the dark night, the light of God's word renders any dark situation insignificant and impotent.

Light is the universal solution to darkness any time, any day and anywhere.

No matter the darkness it bows to light.

You are in the Kingdom of light, so speak the light of His word and not your bad situation or experience.

You are the one speaking into existence; what you have is life. You are the director and captain of your life by your words. The Devil cannot bring anything you did not allow by your word.

The light God gives in your darkness is not ordinary. It is a great light sent to accomplish great things in your life, circumstance, and world.

> *"The people which sat in darkness saw a great light, and to them which sat in the region and shadow of death light is sprung up."* **(Matthew 4:16)**

God bless you. I hope from this day you will begin to speak the beauty that you desire for your life. Do not wait for anyone to do it for you.

CHAPTER 7

Enforcing Your Beauty; Obedience

It is not enough to create your beauty, it must be enforced. You create things with your words and enforce them by your obedience. It is not enough to create your beauty, it must be enforced. Your confession is useless without your obedience; your corresponding action to the word. Any word that is not accompanied by action cannot be enforced. Your action (obedience) gives room for your desires to be established. You are living on a fantasy island with your confession alone. Words alone make you a daydreamer that is building castles in the air. You can confess from now till Jesus returns that "I am rich," but without a corresponding action of diligent labour and sowing into the kingdom you will die poor.

If Jesus only talked about laying down His life and did not do it, Christianity would be a mere fantasy. Many Christians do not have problem with confessing the word but with the doing. Talk is cheap. Everyone can talk. Your confession could be linked to lawmaking and your obedience linked to the police that enforces the law. It does not matter the number of good laws a country might have, they are useless if not enforced by the police. In the same way, your obedience releases power to enforce (plant and establish) your words (desires).

> *"But be ye doers of the word, and not hearers only, deceiving your own selves"* (James 1:22).

Are there oppositions to your desires? I say a big yes, in fact uncountable, but you can have what you say or want by your corresponding action. Hoodlums go aground when policemen show up. In the same, manner, the things opposing your desires go aground when your obedience is in place. In the spiritual realm, obedience is the force that establishes your desire. It is also likened to the price you pay for your goods. It does not matter whether the cashier does not love your face or colour; he will release the goods you desire when you pay for them.

People may consider you unsuitable for what you desire, but that does not matter, once you pay the price it is yours. Obedience delivers to you the deed of ownership. The person in that sleek car may be the least suitable, but if he paid for it, he is qualified to drive it. What am I saying? It does not matter the votes and the opposition against you, once your obedience to the sent word (Faith) is in place, it becomes yours. Your obedience enforces your blessing against all odds. You may not be people's choice for a good job, beautiful marriage, ministry, etc. but once your obedience to the relevant word is in place you enforce it, and it becomes yours.

> *"Yea, though I walk through the valley of the shadow of death, I will fear no evil: for thou art with me; thy rod and thy staff they comfort me. Thou preparest a table before me in the presence of mine enemies: thou anointest my head with oil; my cup runneth over"* **(Psalms 23: 4-5).**

You can have a feast in the valley if the word of God is your companion and you obey it. Your obedience to the word in an unpleasant situation prepares a table for you before your enemies. You can turnaround every ugliness in your life by simple obedience to His word and even come out more anointed. When you are a practitioner of the word, you will always have a table before your enemies.

Your problem is not whether people like you or not, oppose you or not, or wish you bad, your problem is your non-compliance with the word. Once your obedience is in place, you can have it as you wish.

> *"When a man's ways please the LORD, he maketh even his enemies to be at peace with him."* **(Proverbs 16:7)**

Today people are busy looking for who is against them. Let me tell you, as long as you shift focus from yourself; your disobedience to the word, you cannot have your desires. And it will seem like the enemy is more powerful. The enemy is not powerful, you are simply powerless to enforce your desires by your disobedience. Your season of life changes if you act on faith; obey the word. That is why when God wants to bless you He has only you in the picture and directs His word to you. He does not consider people's opinion or action. **(Isaiah 1: 19-20, Deuteronomy 30:15)**

Your beauty is your personal responsibility. Your blessing is not the responsibility of people, their vote, not even that of your pastor's. You are the only one whose vote counts. Cast your vote favourably by your simple obedience. God does not consider people's opinions to bless you, so shield off every person's foolishness by your obedience and make your blessing out of trespass. Obey the word no matter what people do to you or say. Do not let anyone provoke you out of your blessing like they did to Moses.

How Obedience Works

When you obey the word of God, your faith is released and positioned to obtain your desires. *"For by it the elders obtained a good report."* **(Hebrew 11:2)** Obedience to the word releases your faith to obtain your desire from God. If you do not obey, your faith will not be released to obtain your desire. Faith is the incontestable and irresistible force that creates and enforces your desire.

> *"This book of the law shall not depart out of thy mouth; but thou shalt meditate therein day and night, that thou mayest observe to do according to all that is written therein: for then thou shalt make thy way prosperous, and then thou shalt have good success"* (Joshua 1:8).

> *"Now faith is the substance of things hoped for, the evidence of things not seen"* (Hebrews 11:1).

Faith is the force that establishes your desire, it has is no alternative. You cannot receive from God without faith. That is to say, every blessing or promise of God has an accompanying condition you have to obey. Faith is the price tag for every blessing.

> *"As far as your feet tread upon; I give to you"* (Deut. 11:24).

> *"Whatever you lay your hands to do shall prosper"* (Deut. 29:9).

The bible is the land of blessing and promises. And anyone you tread upon by your obedience or you lay your hands to work on is yours. As you tread and work, your faith is released for accomplishment. Nothing can deny you any blessing you tread your feet on and hands to work at. Desires are unrealized if they are only wishes or dreams and not accompanied by action. No matter how you pray, fast, cry, confess, etc. without your hands and legs being involved, putting some action, you will remain where you are. Do whatever the word demands so that you can obtain the increase you desire.

There is profit for every labour (faith and work), but the desire of the slothful (someone that is unwilling to take action) destroys him. Obedience is likened to labour because it is not always easy to do what God demands. The world and circumstances are always against doing the word. I tell you this is labour. And this labour produces faith for profit. Obedience is the spiritual principle God has put in place for your desires. There is always a blessing anytime you obey the word. **(Read James 1:22, Jeremiah 15:16)**

There is a blessing for every word of God you obey. Eat the word for your blessing. Christianity is work; a profession just like every other profession. It is something you should do as a profession whether convenient or not for your livelihood. For the just shall live by Faith. Christianity is your profession; obeying the word whether you feel like it or not.

> *"Man shall live by every word that proceeds from the mouth of God"* **(Matthew 4:4).**

Do you want your Christianity to count, then take every word that proceeds to you from God as a must do; a commandment and not a suggestion. Only then will you begin to enjoy the blessedness of the profession. A doctor works in the hospital because he has to. If he only goes there when he feels like, he will be poor and wretched. In the same way, you should obey the word of God no matter what.

Obedience to the word is your sources of livelihood. Reconsider your choice of Christianity if you are unwilling to obey the word God tells you to obey.

"The just shall live by his Faith" (Habakkuk 2:4).

Do you really want to live? Then obedience is mandatory, not optional. When God says it, do it. Today most Christians are starving, lacking, mourning, etc. because the word is not considered as law. People go to church to be entertained and fulfill a religious obligation and not to get specific instruction to live thereby. Oh, what blessedness if we take our faith as a profession and be diligent with it.

Christianity is demanding just like everything else that profits. Nothing comes easy. If it must profit you, there must be some level of sacrifice. Christianity is work, work of subjecting your flesh to obey the word. It is even more demanding than all secular jobs, but I tell you when you hit the reward, it is better than any pay. Godliness is profitable in all things. The reward of obedience affects the physical and spiritual. Its yields both physical and spiritual profit.

Anytime you do not obey God's word, you lose the blessing it carries. You should as a Christian know that you have been called into a profession. The earlier you realize this the better it is for you. Just like every profession determines the lifestyle of its practitioners, Christianity by the word should tailor your lifestyle. Therefore comply with what the word says.

There is never going to be a time it is convenient to do what the word says, but with caution and practice, you can train your body to adapt to the word all the time. And that is a good exercise for great profit. No one loves to exercise, especially me, and that is why weight is difficult to get rid of. But with determination and training your body adjusts to love and enjoy it even doing it every day. Christianity is exercise unto godliness (obeying the word) for greater profits.

> *"For bodily exercise profiteth little: but godliness is profitable unto all things, having promise of the life that now is, and of that which is to come"* **(1 Timothy 4:8).**

Live Christianity by the word of God that is coming to you per time, and keep at it for enormous profit and reward of great promises. Christianity is not a holy-holy kind of attitude, but submitting yourself to the word of God; being word compliant for your blessing. This is the profession you are called into. On the day you made Jesus your Lord and personal saviour, you traded your will for the will of God; His word in its entirety. How come you are now contending His will? I guess you are ignorant of the profession you signed for.

It is a sheer waste of time going to church or any other place where the word is preached when you are not ready to obey the word that is preached there. God expects you to live by every word as a soldier lives by every order. This is why you cannot afford to be a forgetful hearer, or you will be deceiving yourself. **(Read James 1: 19-24, Luke 6: 46)**

In this profession, every word that proceeds out of the mouth of God to you should be your livelihood; you are expected to act on His word that you heard about the enforcement of your blessing. Enforce those desires of yours by your deliberate choice to obey whatever He says. Choose to obey the word for your good. (Hebrews 4:1-2, 10-11)

When you cease from your own works (ways) and begin to do the works of the word (what God says) you enter into your rest. There is the promise of rest and beauty for you but not without the word. Your compliance with the word enforces your rest and beauty. Check your obedience anytime you are not at rest.

In the kingdom of God, it is not man connection, but Faith connection. Once your obedience is in place, a ladder connects you to Heaven for the delivery (enforcement) of your blessing.

Job was the richest man in his time, and his secret was obedience. **(Job 1:1-3) (Job 29:1-end)**. If you your life must be beautiful, there is no alternative to the word. **(Acts 20:32)** The word builds you up and delivers every blessing God has for you. Your obedience releases the force of Faith that enforces your blessing.

> *"My people are destroyed for lack of knowledge: because thou hast rejected knowledge, I will also reject thee, that thou shalt be no priest to me: seeing thou hast forgotten the law of thy God, I will also forget thy children"* **(Hosea 4:6).**

Let your obedience be intact so that your faith can obtain. Only the doers of the word are blessed. Only the doers of the word are blessed, not the preachers, nor proclaimers. Therefore, if you do any of the above without actually obeying or doing the word you are not blessed, but wasting time and deceiving yourself. Watch out for things that fight the word you hear, they are robbers of your beauty. **(Mark 4: 13-20)**

Take heed not to be a forgetful hearer, but a doer. Keep good notes of messages you have heard and the ones God spoke to you privately, so you can make constant reviews thereby getting the word into your heart. Until the word gets into your heart, you cannot do it.

> *"Thy word have I hid in mine heart, that I might not sin against thee."* **(Psalms 119:11)**

To hide the word means to keep it safe, out of the reach of others or things that might want to steal and destroy it. Enshrine the word in your heart. Do you hide the word in your heart or do you let it depart at the slightest provocation?

> *"Whoever therefore breaks one of the least of these commandments, and teaches men so, shall be called least in the kingdom of heaven; but whoever does and teaches them, he shall be called great in the kingdom of heaven"* **(Matt. 5: 19)**.

Your greatness in the kingdom is a factor of your obedience to the word. Your greatness is directly proportional to your obedience. The words of God are laws, spiritual laws that govern both the spiritual and physical realms. They either affect you negatively or positively depending on your response. In the spiritual, when God speaks, everyone and everything obeys but not so here on earth. Man has free will (choice) to either obey or disobey. Make your choice to obey God. It is in your favour to do so.

My Beautiful Life

CHAPTER 8

Faith Is All It Takes

Do you sometimes wonder how you are going to realize that beautiful life you desire? How will those beautiful and precious promises come to pass? What does it take to live the beautiful life God has designed for you? I have good news for you. FAITH IS ALL IT TAKES. Faith is all it takes to have a beautiful life. Not background, connection, education, weight or anything anyone might think of. In this kingdom, faith is all it takes to obtain whatever you desire; faith and nothing else. There is no alternative to faith if your desires must be realized.

"For the just shall live by faith" (Habakkuk 2:4).

Faith has no alternative so you must have a good understanding of what Faith is. When you understand Faith and live by it, you will realize that beautiful life you desire. Faith's simplest definition is obeying or doing the word of God. The word of God is given to beautify your life. If you obey it, you will experience it. The word of God is the grand design, path, manual and provision for a beautiful life. **(Read 2 Timothy 3:15-16, Joshua 1:8, Psalm 139:15-16, Proverbs 24:13-14).**

Your life has been predestined, and it is in the word. Therefore anytime you obey the word that comes to you, you are unveiling and realizing the beauty God intends for you. **(Act 20:32).** Faith, the doing of the word substantiate what you are hoping.

"Now faith is the [a]substance of things hoped for, the [b] evidence of things not seen" **(Hebrews 11:1).**

Obeying the word delivers to you whatsoever you desire. Note: Faith is obeying the word. The word of God is the will of God. So faith begins when the will of God is known. So faith is in the will of God for you. Anything outside the word of God or Will for you is not faith. Faith can only obtain what is in the word or will of God for you. Anything else that you are believing God for and acting on, if it outside His will for you, it is not genuine faith, but FAKE faith. It is a mere waste of time and resources.

Guard your faith; never have faith outside His will for you. Have real faith and not fake faith. This is where majority miss it. That I saw someone's beautiful car should not make me start having faith for a car; that is covetousness. Faith must begin from the word of God. I must find out God's will for me per time, the provision God has made available for me in His word per time and act on it. Faith comes from the word of God not from seeing what someone has. Faith is borne in you anytime you discover in the word what God has for you. And once faith is in place, and you act, you will have it.

The word of God should determine your faith, not people, the world or circumstances. These may be provocateurs of faith, but actual faith is borne when the word comes. It is not faith to marry someone's husband or wife; that is fake faith. It is not faith to steal without being caught, that is fake. It is not faith to evade responsibility and not bear the consequence of your irresponsibility, that is fake faith. Today because of the prevalence of faith messages, faith has been acted out of context; the context of God's word. And this is the reason many are frustrated and giving up and abandoning faith.

Faith works only in the context of God's word and will for you. Before you set out acting on faith be sure it is founded on the word, only then will it yield results for you. Faith is not bribing God to go beyond His will or word. Rather, faith is pleasing God for your reward. And you can only please God within His word. You can never twist God to act beyond His word. Have you discovered God's will over a matter? Then act accordingly. Otherwise, God will not move. It must be faith not fake faith, for God is no respecter of persons, but in every nation, any man that does His will is acceptable to Him. That means faith work everywhere, even in the harshest country. **(Job 1:1-3, Gen. 12:1-3; 24:1, Matt. 7:24-27, Prov. 24:3-4).**

The house of the righteous is filled with treasures. You can have that beautiful life God has designed for you when you obey the word. When your Faith is in place, you enjoy a beautiful life. Faith is the incontestable force of beauty and excellence. When it is working in your life, you excel. That is you excel when you are doing what God says.

> *"And it shall come to pass, if thou shalt hearken diligently unto the voice of the LORD thy God, to observe and to do all his commandments which I command thee this day, that the LORD thy God will set thee on high above all nations of the earth"* (Deuteronomy 28:1).

Faith makes God break protocol to work for you. Cornelius obedience to God's word brought Peter into the scene. You may not deserve what you need or be qualified for it, but when your obedience is in place, God breaks protocol to provide it. Your obedience engages the host of Heaven on your behalf. Faith is honoured both in Heaven and on Earth.

When the man by the pool of Bethesda was made whole, he did not need any man. When you have Faith; obeying God's word, you do not need man connection. When you have Faith you do not need to run after men for help, God will cause men to work for your good. Your faith is what you need to be made whole and not men. Whatever you need for your life to be made whole is from God not from men. So run after God by your Faith; obedience and men will run after you to meet your needs.

> *"When a man's way pleases the Lord, He makes His enemies at peace with him"* (Psalm 121:1).

Today, many think they have faith in God, but in reality, they have faith in man. Running after men for what they need and taking offense when men fail. If you sincerely have faith in God, you will remove eyes from men, and nothing they do will offend you. When your heart is trusting in God, nothing shall offend you. Then as a wife, you do not take it out on your husband when money is not sufficient. Husband fighting wife and children fighting parents for provision is an indication of misplaced faith. Only God has the power to make whole; to fully satisfy and provide all your needs. No one, but God. Therefore place your faith correctly and enjoy people and things God has provided per time. God is your source, not men. Men are the means God uses, and He can use anyone. So fix your eyes on God; the source.

No one receives anything apart from what is given to him from above (God).

"Every good and perfect gift comes from God" (James 1:17).

Placing faith in men makes you men pleaser or men accuser (when they fail). Are you always trying to please men or finding fault? Then you might have placed your faith wrongly. There is a sister that God has used marvelously to supply my clothes several times. Another time I needed a change of wardrobe, rather than ask her, I told God. After three days, God miraculously changed my wardrobe through someone I did not even know. Those were beautiful dresses I tell you. I would have limited myself if I had asked the sister and denied God the glory.

Run after God by obeying the word, and men will run after you to please you; this is rest. Once the relevant word comes to you and you obey it, it becomes your turn for your desire to be met. Labour to please God and not men. Embrace the word through your obedience and take hold of what it delivers to you. Do you desire a husband or wife? It does not matter how unqualified you are, only find the word and do it, and not too long you will be celebrating your wedding. A good wife or husband comes from the Lord. So be willing to obey God; the word He has laid in your heart, and you will be qualified. God will bypass every protocol and take you to your man or wife.

This is the principle of faith; finding the word of God and doing it for your desire. This principle applies to every desire of yours. For whatsoever you desire, find the right word, obey it, and God will honour your Faith by releasing your desire. Please God by your Faith and the blessing shall be yours. Promotion does not come from the north or south, but from God. Do not please men at the expense of God or you lose out. When your ways please the Lord, He might even use your enemies to work for you. Love people, respect them, enjoy them, but do not put your trust in them or commit yourself to please them.

> *"But Jesus did not commit Himself to them, because He knew all men, and had no need that anyone should testify of man, for He knew what was in man" (John 2:24-25 NKJV).*

No man has the power to meet your need except God touches him. Never assume the place of God in anyone's life, or you will be drained. You cannot do everything for someone nor be everything to him. Do not be deceived to think you are indispensable. Faith work is realistic for those that seek him shall find Him. Faith is realistic and attainable but not mysterious. It is substantial. It's got proofs.

> *"Neither say they in their heart, let us now fear the LORD our God, that giveth rain, both the former and the latter, in his season: he reserveth unto us the appointed weeks of the harvest"* **(Jeremiah 5:24).**

> *"For he performeth the thing that is **appointed for me: and many such things are with him"*** **(Job 23:14).**

The fear of God is coming afresh on you, and you shall not miss any week that is reserved for your harvest. If Faith is all it takes, then only God matters for your beautiful life.

In summary, read Job22:21-30 in the next page. Keep the faith principle, and your life will be beautified. And only what is impossible with God is impossible in your life. Remember death, lack, sickness, etc., is not in your beautiful life.

"Now acquaint yourself with Him, and be at peace; Thereby good will come to you. Receive, please, instruction from His mouth, And lay up His words in your heart. If you return to the Almighty, you will be built up; You will remove iniquity far from your tents. Then you will lay your gold in the dust, And the gold of Ophir among the stones of the brooks. Yes, the Almighty will be your [a]gold And your precious silver; For then you will have your delight in the Almighty, And lift up your face to God. You will make your prayer to Him, He will hear you, And you will pay your vows. You will also declare a thing, And it will be established for you; So light will shine on your ways. When they cast you down, and you say, 'Exaltation will come!' Then He will save the humble person. He will even deliver one who is not innocent; Yes, he will be delivered by the purity of your hands" (Job 22:21-30 NKJV).

CHAPTER 9

Faith Antagonist 1: Hindrances To Beauty

Before you start this chapter, I want you to know there is no limit to your beautiful life. There is no limit to the extent God can bless you. You are the one that sets limit by your faith. This chapter is so important for you to identify the things that oppose your faith and resist them; thereby taking the limits off your beautiful life. When you deal with these Faith Antagonists, your life will be beautiful beyond your wildest imagination.

> *"But as it is written: Eye has not seen, nor ear heard, Nor have entered into the heart of man, the things which God has prepared for those who love Him"* **(1 Corinthians 2: 9 -10).**

When you take off brakes from what the Spirit reveals to you, your beautiful life will have no limit. You are beautified to the extent of your Faith. Uncompromising faith brings unlimited blessing. By Faith Antagonists I mean the things that oppose your Faith, things that compete with your Faith for the same ground. Faith is a product of the word in the heart. Faith binds with the heart and produces action in you. These faith antagonists, just like the word bind with the heart, prevent faith from binding and producing.

If you did science, these faith antagonists function like enzyme antagonists competing with specific enzyme for its binding site on a substrate, thereby hindering or alternating the enzyme function and activity. Identifying these faith antagonists will enable you to overcome them so that faith can bind with the heart and work fruitfully for your beautiful life.

Every born again child of God is called to a Faith walk; to a life of Faith. *"For the just shall live by Faith."* **(Habakkuk 2:4)** Once you become a Christian, you have automatically registered to a life of Faith walkers, and you are expected to walk to the end. If the Faith walk (work) is easy, how come not everyone gets to the finish line?

Paul admonishes us to fight the good fight of Faith.

> *"Fight the good fight of faith, lay hold on eternal life, to which you were also called and have confessed the good confession in the presence of many witnesses"* **(1 Timothy 6:12).**

If Paul describes faith as a fight, that means it is not a bread and butter affair, it is hard work, with resistance and oppositions that you need to fight and press through to obtain. It is sad that many Christians are unaware of this and handle their faith leisurely. If you must succeed and obtain your beautiful life, you must understand that faith is a fight. From the moment you receive Jesus, oppositions arise to prevent your Faith from gaining ground and becoming productive. I have good news for you; even though faith is a fight, it is a good fight. This means that if you care to fight, you will win. The fight of faith will always turn out in your favour. **(Read 1 Corinthian 9:24-27).**

There is the promise of God's kind of life at the finishing line, a life of abundant blessing. Zoe life talks about the eternal life Christ died to give us as believers. It affects the present life and that which is to come. It is the life of peace, joy, and righteousness. This is just a glimpse of your beautiful life. As you go through this chapter, allow God to open your eyes to identify what easily hinders your Faith; your obedience to the word. And these are the things that hinder your experience of the fullness of God's promises in your spirit, soul, and body.

When you identify them, believe God to heal you and make His grace abound towards you to overcome them. What hinders you may be different from another person. After this chapter, nothing shall be able to hinder you; you will run to the finish line and obtain your glorious promises. I plead the blood of Jesus on you for a new heart that embraces Faith.

The blood of Jesus shall speak strength in every way you have been hindered.

> **"Ye did run well; who did hinder you that ye should not obey the truth?" (Galatian 5:7).**

I plead the blood against whatsoever that have hindered you. You shall pass over in Jesus mighty name. God, through this chapter, will raise a standard for you against every obstacle of the wicked for you to run, run, and run.

I want to share something God revealed to me in **John 4: 49-53.** Jesus spoke the word, and the man obeyed and left; that is Faith. Faith is putting your confidence or trust in what Jesus says, so much that it precipitates your corresponding actions. Anytime you act on what Jesus says (word of God), you obtain God's kind of life; the supernatural. Supposing the man argued with Jesus and did not obey immediately, he would not have received that miracle.

How many times has Jesus spoken the word to you; the Holy Spirit inspires you to do something, and you did nothing about it. That is not faith. Moreover, you are denied that miracle associated with that prompted word. Notice from the above scripture that it was the same hour Jesus spoke that the boy was healed. I want you to know that whenever God says something about your situation, it is done at that time. All you need is to add the corresponding action to experience it. In other words, when you have or hear God's word concerning issues, it is already done. And from that moment when you got the word, God is expecting and waiting for you to act on the word for the physical manifestation. The ball is in your court after you have heard the word. What you do with the word determines the outcome.

You only wait on God till the word comes. After you got the word; run with the word. Waiting on God from thence is a mere waste of time. Anything that deters you from acting on the word denies your blessing. Many for lack of action have made it seem like this "Faith thing" is not working. People's negligence makes the word seem unproductive. These are the people Paul describes as;

> *"Having a form of godliness but have denied the power thereof"* (2 Timothy 3:5).

They claim to be born again; go to church, but refuse to do the word. Thereby denying themselves the power of Faith that makes the word to work with proofs. Faith is the power that makes the word effective.

Faith makes the word work. God cannot work for you without your faith, your obedience to His word, no matter how much you cry, whine and complain. Do not be deceived by what it looks like, the word of God works. The word is alive and active.

> *"Faith without work is dead"* (James 2:17).

What makes your Faith alive and productive is your work

(actions of obedience). On this note, not all professed Faith is alive. Some have dead Faith and some living Faith. But only living Faith; Faith backed up with actions, obtains the beautiful life.

Not all have living Faith, so do not expect all to have proofs. **(Hebrews 4:2-4)** This is why you should never use people's experience to judge the integrity of God's word nor base your decision on it. God is true to His word. He means what He says and says what He means in His word. He is not a liar **(Numbers 23:19).** No one should be your yardstick. Not even all preachers work the word. That is why experiences of God's Faithfulness vary from one preacher to the other. So examine those that preach the word to you and choose whose Faith to imitate. The word is no respecter of persons; you must work it, for it to work for you.

> *"Then Peter opened his mouth, and said, Of a truth I perceive that God is no respecter of persons"* **(Acts 10:34).**

Though I am a minister of the word, I am not excused from obeying the word. I pay my tithe, and the ministry pays also, and God has been true to His word. Paul said,

> *"I bring myself under subjection so that after I have preached to others, I shall not be a castaway"* **(1 Corinthians 9:27).**

Subject yourself to the word regardless of your feelings or opinion. There may be many logical excuses, but choose to obey the word anyway. If the man by Bethesda Pool had considered his excuses, he would not have obeyed and would have died paralyzed **(John 5)**. Obey the word, act on it, even if you might need help. Faith always works for people that work the word.

Why must you obey the word to get what you need? It shows you are really earnest about what you desire. God does not waste His blessing or resources on people that do not really desire them. If you are willing to be committed to something by your action, it shows you are interested in it, and God will show Himself forth. If you earnestly desire it, you will do something about it. Proverbs says hunger in a man's belly makes his hands to work. If your heart is in it, you will go for it. If you give and entertain excuses, you are not in need of it yet.

"The person who labors, labors for himself, for his hungry mouth drives him on" **(Proverbs 16:26)**.

Excuses

One major hindrance or antagonist to Faith is **EXCUSES**. The paralysed man and his friends in Mark 2 had many reasons not to obtain healing from Jesus, but they refused even to the extent of removing somebody's house roof to get to Jesus. Nothing could stand in the way of their Faith. What about the woman with the issue of blood? She went to great lengths to reach Jesus, breaking all social norms Ask Zacchaeus; he had to shun his reputation, ridicule, small status, shame and so on, to climb the sycamore tree to see Jesus. The reason your faith is hindered is that you are not desperate enough to shun obstacles and excuses on your path of faith. You turn back at the least opposition and give flimsy excuses.

Desperation accompanies Faith with action. Desperation makes you obey the word whether it makes sense or not. Until your situation gets desperate, you will still be considering whether to obey the word or not. That is why Faith is seen as the last resort, rather than the way of life. God is not a standby generator or a magician. He is your Father and wants to be involved in your life. He longs for a full-time relationship with you, by your obedience to His word. He wants to be involved in your life by His word. Do not wait until the situation is desperate to obey and let Him in. Any excuse you entertain denies God's involvement in your life.

Procrastination

Another hindrance to Faith is procrastination. That is putting off action to a later time. This attitude hinders faith because faith is in the NOW. If it's not NOW, it's no faith. The word that comes to you demands certain actions immediately; in the now not later. **In John 5: 8-9,** the man was asked to pick up his mat, and he did immediately. When Elisha told the widow to pour the oil into the vessel she went and did it immediately. When God speaks a word to you, you must begin to affect it now. There is no more convenient time to do what God is telling you, now is the time, so do not postpone it.

> *"Now faith is the [a]substance of things hoped for, the [b]*
> *evidence of things not seen"* **(Hebrews 11:1 NKJV).**

How many times have you heard God's word for your healing and rather than acting immediately, you push it up for next time? "I know God will heal me someday." If you believe God will heal you someday why not today? If you do not believe God will heal you now but some other day that's not faith. You are only hoping to be healed someday. This is different from the faith that says; I am healed by the stripes of Jesus. I doubt if you actually believed. I wonder why someday, will God grow stronger? If God will not grow stronger, and His power is same forever, what is stopping you from being healed today? Doubt and unbelief!

Any Faith in the future is camouflaged unbelief and not Faith. Faith is now. Someone would say "I believe I will speak in tongues someday." I ask the same question, why not today and now? Procrastination is a ploy of the enemy to hinder you from acting on what you believe for your blessing. If he succeeds in making you push your action forward, he has hindered your Faith. The Devil is not bold enough to stop you from believing God can do it, but he comes subtly to prevent your action in the now.

Today as you are reading this, I declare you healed, filled with the Holy Spirit, prosperous. Today you are made whole. I break every satanic ploy of procrastination against your Faith. I render them ineffective to stop them from acting on God's word now. There is no day called tomorrow or someday. God only has one day to work and do miracles and that day is today.

"Today if you hear His voice harden not your heart..."
(Hebrews 3:15).

Do what He tells you today now and enjoy the work He has done for you. Now is the acceptable time, obey his word now. Rise up from that sick bed and live. Your Faith works for you now, today not tomorrow or someday.

My beloved of the Lord, please, be cautious of excuses and procrastination, they displaces faith in your heart and renders it ineffective.

CHAPTER 10

Faith Antagonists II

In the previous chapter, I explained things that can hinder your faith and thereby limit your beauty. These are EXCUSES and PROCRASTINATION. In this chapter, I will explain a few more. These are not conclusive on things that hinder faith, there are many more. Anything that stops you from obeying the word of God falls into this category and would limit your beauty. The list is endless. In this last chapter, I will point out few that Jesus mentioned in the Parable of the Sower **(Read Mark 4: 13-20).**

Before I go on, I would like to mention the phases of Faith in which these oppositions could occur. Faith has three phases or stages, and these stages experience different oppositions. At whatever level the opposition occurs, it hinders your Faith:

(1) Getting Faith (2) Receiving Faith (3) Doing Faith.

Getting Faith Related Oppositions

"Faith cometh by hearing and hearing the word of God"
(Romans 10:17).

NOTE: Hearing is a continuous term. Yesterday hearing does not guarantee today's Faith. You have to constantly hear the word of God to keep the Faith. Therefore anything that prevents you from hearing, reading or studying the word hinders your Faith, and it prevents Faith from gaining access to you. Advanced technology is a major distraction from the word. There have been increased distractions from hearing the word. So many distractions prevent you from sitting with the word.

Technology has advanced and brought various distractions ranging from Internet, television, social media like Facebook, the cell phone, texting, etc. Even the audio bible has not been a good substitute for studying the word. We spend time with these and do not find time for the word. I have decided not to trade my personal time with the word for anything. Everything else can wait, but not the word.

Nothing should substitute the time you devoted to reading and studying the word (The Bible) in your devotional time. No matter how good a book or devotional is, it should not replace the Bible during your word time. There is nothing that can be compared with the life (faith) that emanates from the word. Other books should be complementary and not substitutes to the infallible word of God that has the ability to deliver to you, your inheritance.

Listening to your audio Bible cannot be substituted for studying the word. If you have time to take food and put in your mouth, you should have time to sit down and fix your eyes on the word and study. This involves some level of discipline. If a student is not disciplined to sit and study he will not pass the exam. If a student is wise to do some studying before an ordinary exam, you should be wiser to get down with the word to get Faith to pass the exam of life. Surely there will always be challenges in life you must pass. Friends could also hinder you from the word. Fast these things that interfere with your word time.

Cut down the amount of time you spend on Facebook, the Internet, phones, etc. Anything that stops you from going where the word is preached prevents you from hearing the word and hinders your Faith. This includes such things as social visits, work schedule, laziness, and leisure among many others. Nothing should be strong enough to stop you from constantly engaging the word.

"Man shall live by every word that proceeds out of the mouth of God" (Matthew 4:4).

Your real life is in the word. You are not actually living any day until you get the word. The word is the life of your spirit which is the real you. Without the word impacting your life, you will be weighed down, irritated, depressed and overwhelmed.

When you access the word at the beginning of each day, real life comes to you and you are set for the day. And no challenge can put you down.

> *"They call them gods unto whom the word has come"* **(John 10:35).**

The word translates you to god level and experience.

Receiving The Word Related Opposition

After you get the word, you are expected to receive it; accept it into your heart and make it part of you. These antagonists operate at the heart level. They occupy the heart and prevent the word you heard from been planted there. Until you receive the word, you will not be able to do it and reap the benefits. These oppositions prevent the word from being planted. Not every listener of the word actually hears and receives the word. Hearing is of the heart; receiving the word into the heart.

The Parable of the Sower (**Mark 4: 13-20**) enumerates things that can prevent one from receiving the word.

Satan

Jesus likened the seeds that fell on the roadside as those that heard but did not understand and Satan came immediately and stole the word. The chief opposition to the word is Satan. Satan steals the word and prevents it from being planted. Satan is so antagonistic to your receiving the word because he knows as soon as Faith is borne in you, you have overcome.

"What is it that overcomes the world, even your Faith" (**1 John 5:4**).

Devil is no match for you when you have Faith. Note as soon as the word was sown, he **immediately** stole it. Permit me to say he is always at the point of receiving the word. Therefore be careful how you hear. When the message is preached, avoid distraction, or you will lose it. How you hear connotes your attitude. Give total attention to the word.

Rocks

The seed that fell on rocky hearts did not have much earth, and they died. Rocks in the heart prevent the word from full maturity. Rocks signify pride, tradition, self-will, ideas, etc. Rocks are symbolic of things that over the years have been part of the heart. If the word will be planted and blossom unto fruitfulness, you must break up the fallow ground. Break it up. It is you that will do it. Change your ideas, way of life, imagination, etc. If you follow the word, you must deny yourself, discard your ways. Pride would have stopped Naaman (**2 Kings 5**) from receiving the word for his miracle. Allow the word to change you.

Tradition would have prevented healing on the Sabbath day. God's word supersedes every tradition and custom. Accept the word even when it is contrary to your tradition. Traditions of men have made the word less effective. Traditions could mean how you do things.

Religion

Religion constitutes a major rock in the heart that hinders the word. Religion is man's way (idea) to God and is different from Christianity, God's way (idea) to man. They might sound the same, but there are great differences. Religion can never take anyone to God because no one comes to Him except He draws the person to Himself.

> *"No one can come to Me unless the Father who sent Me draws him; and I will raise him up at the last day"* (John 6:44).

There is never a way man can get to God through his way (religion). You must approach God by His way as revealed in the word. Religion takes the place of the word in the hearts of men that practice it, and make them feel they are with God, while they are very far from Him. With the lips they honour God, but their hearts are far from Him.

> *"This people draweth nigh unto me with their mouth and honoureth me with their lips, but their heart is far from me. But in vain they do worship me, teaching for doctrines the commandments of men"* (Matthew 15:8-9).

What a deceit religion is to people. Men in an attempt to create a way to God have believed things contrary to the word. They have not only believed it themselves but have taught others the same preventing the word a place in their hearts. Faith is borne in a religious person as long as it goes with what he had been thought, anything beyond that is not for him. And this hinders his Faith. Though most religions seem harmless, they have robbed people of their Faith and blessing.

Be careful, do not be religious, be a Christian. Get to God the way He has set in His word. Religion is a stealer and killer. Sometimes religion creeps into Pentecostal worship and steals the word. Long ago, I made up my mind not to allow Anglicanism to deny me any of my blessings in the word. Though my Father was an Anglican Clergy; I set out to obtain whatever the word has for me. I would do whatever the word says regardless of my family position. I would speak in tongues, get baptized by inversion and would go witnessing.

Are you a Christian or religionist? Mirror your church teaching and doctrine by the word and decide your faith. The one you accept fully determines your Faith. It is impossible to have faith in the word and in your religion, that is, it is impossible to believe whatever your religion teaches and do all that the word says. Matthew 6:24 says, you cannot serve two masters at a time. You will have preferred loyalty above the other.

> *"No one can serve two masters; for either he will hate the one and love the other, or else he will be loyal to the one and despise the other. You cannot serve God and [a]mammon."*

Similarly, Matthew 9:17says neither can put new wine in an old wineskin.

> *"Nor do they put new wine into old wineskins, or else the wineskins [a]break, the wine is spilled, and the wineskins*

are ruined. But they put new wine into new wineskins, and both are preserved."

Choose one. For me, I choose Christianity; Christ's way as shown in the word. Religion will not give me all I need nor make me all that God has designed me to be here and after, but the word would.

Christianity simply means Christ-like. Jesus, when He was on earth, lived by the word of God and abhorred religion. He was hated by the religious people. Whatever God told him He did and whatever He saw God do, He did. Jesus broke religious standard in His earthly days. If Jesus had clung unto religion and the law, He would not have done all that God had designed Him to do. He healed on the Sabbath, talked with the adulterous woman, dined with sinners, ate with unwashed hands, etc. Jesus was God person, not a religious person. Make your choice today. Come out of the shell of religion and be all that God has for you, radiating your beautiful life.

"All Scripture is given by inspiration of God, and is profitable for doctrine, for reproof, for correction, for [a]instruction in righteousness, that the man of God may be complete, thoroughly equipped for every good work" (2 Timothy 3: 16-17).

Do not be limited in your work of Faith. Religion would have stopped the man that Jesus healed by the pool of Bethesda, but he shunned religion carried his mat and walked in the beauty of his healing.

"The Jews, therefore, said unto him that was cured, it is the sabbath day: it is not lawful for thee to carry thy bed. He answered them, He that made me whole, the same said unto me, Take up thy bed, and walk" (John 5:10-11).

Why have you allowed religion to stop you from obeying the word and becoming all that God has created you to be? Will you do what Jesus says in the word by his rules or what religion says? Anything I see in the word I do, I cannot be bound by any religion. Religion is anti-miracle and anti-wonders. Religious people greatly opposed Jesus so be ready for a fight if you decide to break forth. Get set to put up a fight if you choose the word.

Religion hates it when you say that God is your Father and that you have a personal relationship with Him because it has never succeeded to get anyone to that point. They wanted to stone Jesus to death because He said God was His Father. Religion will always want to put something or someone between you and God; either an object or person living or dead and says things like "You cannot pray directly to God, you have to go through Mary or Angels." "You must say a certain prayer in a certain season and the certain way" and encourages the use of chaplet.

I ask, where is the place of the Holy Spirit in all these? Religion demeans the work of the Holy Spirit who reveals all that is yours in Christ; that also teaches and guides you into all truth.

> *"However, when He, the Spirit of truth, has come, He will guide you into all truth; for He will not speak on His own authority, but whatever He hears He will speak; and He will tell you things to come"*(John 16:13).

You have been redeemed as saints unto God; as Jesus is God's son. And no one stands between the Father and the Son. Jesus has made direct access to the Father and has brought you into this close union. Father and Son relationship is the closest ever. Not only does the son have the Father's nature and likeness, but he also abides in the house forever. This sonship position offers to you unbelievable right and confidence. The son has as much glory and beauty as the father.

This is what religion deprives people. Religion denies you the confidence to operate in amazing faith. The son has the right that the Father has, unlimited Faith. The Son has access to all that he the Father has; God's kind of Faith.

> *"But as many as received Him, to them He gave the [a]right to become children of God, to those who believe in His name"* (John1: 12).

With every apology to your feeling, Mary is no go between you and God. I did not write it; it is in the Bible.

> *"Jesus saith unto him, I am the way, the truth, and the life: no man cometh unto the Father, but by me"* (John 14:6).

You are not Mary's Child, but God's Child. If you have received Jesus as your Lord, you are God's Child through Jesus, and you have direct access to Him.

> *"Therefore being justified by faith, we have peace with God through our Lord Jesus Christ: By whom also we have access by faith into this grace wherein we stand, and rejoice in hope of the glory of God"* **(Romans 5:1-2).**

Many that could have been doing great exploits by their Faith as sons are limited by religion and are bound by a slave mentality. No matter how a servant is loved, he does not have as much right, Faith and confidence as the Son. You cannot compare Faith operation from Sonship level with that of the servant level. These are two quite different perspectives.

> *"I have said, Ye are gods; and all of you are children of the most High. But ye shall die like men, and fall like one of the princes"* **(Psalm 82: 6-7).**

Do not allow religion to get your Faith to the level of a servant; beggarly. You are Jesus' brother, Friend and you owe everything the Father has with Him. It is your right by position.

> *"But now, after that ye have known God, or rather are known of God, how turn ye again to the weak and beggarly elements, whereunto ye desire again to be in bondage?* **(Galatians 4:9).**

Discard religion and embrace friendship with Jesus and discover the mysteries of the word of great Faith.

"I do not call you servant but friends, because everything I know I show to you" (John 15:15).

Friends are entitled to Kingdom mysteries. Religion prevents you from reading the word to explore secrets. It gives you other books than the bible to read. It tells you a certain way and things to do and pray thereby limiting your sonship experience.

I choose to be led by the Spirit because He knows the will and mind of the Father for me and helps me to please God. Religion puts a ceiling on you. Follow the word and your mind will be blown away. **(Read John 5:30, Colossians 2:8-11, 22-23).**

Take personal responsibility to discover God in His word and shun anything that is contrary. Do not push this responsibility to someone else. When you sincerely desire to do His will, you will seek for it, and nothing can stop you. "

If any man will do his will, he shall know of the doctrine, whether it be of God, or whether I speak of myself" (John 7:17).

Religion is cloak people use not to obey God. They hide under the cloak of religion. Everything that should be known of God is plain in His word. Search the scripture and have life indeed.